THE
BAKING
COOKBOOK

THE
BAKING
COOKBOOK

From the oven to the table

This edition published in 2011
LOVE FOOD is an imprint of Parragon Books Ltd

Parragon
Queen Street House
4 Queen Street
Bath BA1 1HE, UK

ISBN: 978-1-4454-4326-3

Printed in China

Cover artwork by Georgina Luck, www.georginaluck.com

Notes for the Reader

This book uses imperial, metric, and US cup measurements. Follow the same units of measurement throughout; do not mix imperial and metric. All spoon measurements are level: teaspoons are assumed to be 5 ml, and tablespoons are assumed to be 15 ml. Unless otherwise stated, milk is assumed to be whole, individual vegetables such as potatoes are medium, eggs are large, and pepper is freshly ground black pepper.

The times given are an approximate guide only. Preparation times differ according to the techniques used by different people and the cooking times may also vary from those given as a result of the type of oven used. Optional ingredients, variations, or serving suggestions have not been included in the calculations.

Recipes using raw or very lightly cooked eggs should be avoided by infants, the elderly, pregnant women, convalescents, and anyone with a chronic condition. Pregnant and breastfeeding women are advised to avoid eating peanuts and peanut products. People with nut allergies should be aware that some of the prepared ingredients used in the recipes in this book may contain nuts. Always check the packaging before use.

Picture acknowledgments

The publisher would like to thank Getty Images for permission to publish copyright material on the following pages: Page 2: full page 102280550 Pie on kitchen stone by Rick Lew, page 5: full page 72801446 Baking tin with pastry & vanilla cream, red currants on skimmer by Foodcollection, page 6–7: double page 56296076 Rye flour by Teubner, page 8–9: double page 89804103 Assortment of pies by Judd Pilossof, page 10–11: 10 x 15 cm 91616676 Flour, butter and rubber spatula in mixing bowl, close-up, view from above by Tina Rupp, page 12: 7 x 18 cm 56166275 Woman baking in kitchen, Image Source, page 15: full page 78807367 Stack of Pie Pans with One Pie Crust by Fuse, page 25: full page 73441922 Heart-shaped cookie cutters on floured board by Foodcollection, page 26: 10.5 x 11 cm 90545604 Assorted breads and bread rolls in bread basket by Foodcollection RF, page 32–33: double page 87319063 Woman making a cake by Image Source, page 70–71: double page 102675605 Woman holding tray of cupcakes by Tara Moore, page 108–109: double page 80356518 Teenaged girl baking cookies by Tetra Images, page 146–147: double page 74353123 Hands rolling out pastry by Angie Norwood Browne, page 184–185: double page 71578472 Flour and yeast for baking bread by Axel Weiss

CONTENTS

Chapter 4: Sweet Pies & Pastries 146

Chapter 5: Bread & Savory 184

Index 222

Introduction

Equipment

Oven

A reliable oven is essential to successful baking, and it's a good idea to check yours regularly with an oven thermometer to make sure it's accurate. Preheat the oven to the required temperature for 10–15 minutes before use, so that it has time to fully reach the correct temperature. Convection ovens cook more quickly than conventional ovens, so cooking times can be reduced by 5–10 minutes per hour, or the temperature may be reduced slightly. Avoid the temptation to keep opening the oven door to check on your cake, particularly early in the cooking time, because a sudden rush of cold air may cause the cake to sink.

Measuring Cups

Metal and ceramic measuring cups are useful for measuring dry ingredients but less easy to use for liquids. Transparent glass or plastic cups are a good choice for measuring liquids, but make sure that they are heatproof. Choose ones with a good pouring lip and clear markings. Place the cup on a flat surface at eye level for accurate measuring of liquid ingredients.

Dry measuring cups are available in nested sets and usually include 1-cup, ½-cup, ⅓-cup, and ¼-cup sizes. Although soft butter and margarine and brown sugar should be packed tightly into a measuring cup, all other ingredients should be placed into a measuring cup loosely. Unless otherwise stated, the ingredients in the cups should be level—you can use the straight back edge of a knife or your fingers to level off the ingredients.

Measuring Spoons

It's important to use standard measuring spoons, measured level unless stated otherwise, because ordinary kitchen tablespoons and teaspoons can vary in size. A standard set of measuring spoons includes ¼ teaspoon, ½ teaspoon, 1 teaspoon, and 1 tablespoon.

Electric Mixer/Food Processor

A handheld electric mixer with a powerful motor can be used for creaming, whisking, blending, and kneading. Tabletop mixers, with greater capacity and more power, are useful for all mixtures, particularly large quantities. Food processors can cream, blend, or knead, as well as doing other cooking tasks. Again, choose one with a powerful motor for durability. Be careful when using a food processor or powerful electric mixer for making cakes because they mix the ingredients very quickly. It is important not to overbeat cake batters because this will make their texture too dense. Food processors are unsuitable for mixing meringues because the enclosed bowl does not hold enough air to give them volume.

Spoons

Wooden spoons are useful for creaming and mixing. Make sure you keep separate those used for cooking strongly flavored foods, such as onions, because wood can absorb flavors and may transfer them to more delicate mixtures. Heat-resistant nylon spoons are durable and less prone to absorbing flavors. A large metal spoon is useful for folding in ingredients.

Spatula

You'll find a flexible rubber or silicone spatula helpful for light mixing and scraping out bowls cleanly. Some have a spoon-shape blade, which helps when transferring cake batter from the bowl to the pan.

Bowls

Mixing bowls in different sizes are essential, and a set of toughened glass bowls is a good basic start because they are durable, heatproof, and easy to clean. Melamine resin, plastic, and ceramic bowls often have pouring lips, and some have nonslip bottoms to grip the surface.

Wire Cooling Racks

A wire rack lets your cakes cool evenly and prevents condensation, which can cause soggy texture and poor keeping quality. They vary from a simple metal rectangle to expanding three-tier ones, which are useful for large batches of baking. Some have a nonstick coating for easier cleaning.

Sifter/Strainer

A good-quality rustproof metal sifter with a triggerlike handle or crank is useful for sifting together dry ingredients evenly. Or use a stainless steel or nylon strainer, which sometimes come in a set of three. These are also useful for separating liquids and solids. Even nylon ones are hard wearing and will stand boiling water, but metal ones are the most durable and will last for years.

Graters

A hard-wearing stainless steel box grater or flat "Microplane"-style type grater with a firm grip handle are good for grating citrus rind, cheese, apple, chocolate, nutmeg, etc. You'll need a fine, medium, and coarse grater. Some also have a slicing option.

Citrus Squeezer/Reamer

A sturdy plastic, metal, toughened glass, or ceramic squeezer is used for extracting juice from citrus fruits. For smooth juice, you'll need one with a filter part to extract all the fibers from the juice. A wooden reamer squeezes out the juice by simply pushing into the halved fruit, but you may also get some seeds.

Rolling Pin

For rolling pie and cookie doughs, a wooden rolling pin is a good tool and you can shape and cool tuiles on it, too. Marble, granite, or glass are more expensive but their cool smooth surface is good for rolling sticky mixtures.

Pastry Brush

A pastry brush is the easiest way to grease cake pans evenly, and can also be used for applying glazes. They are available with natural bristles or more durable synthetic bristles.

Cookie Cutters

A set of round cookie cutters, with either plain or fluted edges, is a good basic choice, preferably in metal. Later you can add cutters in fancy shapes. Make sure the cutting edge is sharp and the top edge is rolled to safeguard your fingers and keep the cutter rigid.

Pastry Bag and Tips

For decorative piping of frostings or soft mixtures, you'll need pastry bags and tips. Strong nylon or fabric bags are washable and reusable, or you can buy strong disposable bags to save work. A small selection of stainless steel tips should include a plain writing, small and large star, and plain large tips.

Ingredients

Flour

Wheat flour is the most commonly used flour for baking. The amount of gluten (protein) in wheat flour varies between the different types:

All-purpose flour has the bran and wheat germ removed, and is then fortified with vitamins. Soft all-purpose flour is made from wheat with a low-gluten content. It has a fine texture and is ideal for making cakes, pie dough, and cookies. White bread flour is milled from wheat with a high-gluten content and is used for breads and most yeast cooking.

Self-rising flour is all-purpose white flour with a leavening agent. To make self-rising flour add 1½ teaspoons of baking powder plus ½ teaspoon of salt to each 1 cup all-purpose flour.

Whole wheat flour is flour that has been milled from the whole of the wheat grain. It is coarser and heavier than white flour. It is available as a strong (high-gluten) flour for bread making and a soft (lower-gluten) flour for cakes and pastry.

Other flours, such as malted flour, corn flour, and buckwheat, rye, rice, and chestnut flours, are also sometimes used to a limited extent in baking, each having its own unique characteristic or flavor.

Sugars

Most sugar is produced from one of two sources: sugar cane or sugar beet. There are a number of different types of sugar, each with its own particular qualities. Unrefined sugars are made from sugar cane and have a higher mineral, vitamin, and trace element content than refined sugars.

Granulated sugar can be used to achieve a crunchy texture in some cookies and in cakes prepared by the rubbing-in method.

Superfine sugar has a finer crystal and dissolves more readily. It is a good choice for baking because it dissolves readily. It is suitable for placing in a caster—a container with a perforated top, similar to a flour sifter. Because it dissolves readily, it is perfect for making meringues. It can be substituted for granulated sugar cup for cup. If you don't have superfine sugar on hand, you can process an equivalent amount of granulated sugar in a food processor or blender for 1 minute.

Raw brown sugar is a large, coarse-grained brown sugar that can be made from either refined or unrefined sugar. As well as being used in baking, it is sometimes sprinkled over the tops of pies, crumbles, and cakes for its crunchy texture.

Light and **dark brown sugars** are usually refined white sugar that has been tossed in molasses or syrup. The darker the sugar, the stronger the molasses flavor.

Confectioners' sugar, sometimes called powdered sugar, has a fine,

powdery grain and dissolves almost instantly. It is used in some cookies and pastry, and for making frostings and fillings.

Other sugar forms include sugar cubes, which are solid blocks of sugar that can be crushed and used for adding texture and decorating cakes and cookies. You can also use rock sugar (or Chinese rock sugar, yellow rock sugar, and other variations of these names) in a similar manner. Decorating, or coarse, sugar, has granules that are about four times larger than normal granulated sugar; it can be found in specialty cake shops and is used for decoration.

Fats

Butter produces the best flavor. Unsalted butter is generally considered best for baking. If you do use salted butter, you will not need to add any extra salt to the recipe (except for bread making). Use butter straight from the refrigerator for pastry making and at room temperature for cake making.

Margarine is preferred over butter by some people for baking. Block margarine is generally the best to use, but soft margarine is needed when making cakes by the all-in-one method.

Low-fat spreads are not suitable for baking, because they contain a high proportion of water.

Lard is used for making biscuits and pastry. It's made from pork fat and is usually processed, which not only makes it firmer but also creates a milder flavor.

Vegetable shortening has a bland flavour, but produces a light, short texture to pastry and cookies, so is sometimes used. It is usually combined with butter for flavor.

Eggs

The size of eggs used in baking is important. Store eggs in the refrigerator away from strong-smelling foods. Remove from the refrigerator to return to room temperature before using if

possible, because cold eggs do not combine as well with other ingredients or trap as much air.

Leavening Agents

Baking powder is a mixture of cream of tartar and baking soda. When mixed with moisture, it releases carbon dioxide, a harmless gas that expands during baking to make the food rise.

Baking soda produces carbon dioxide when mixed with an acid, such as lemon juice or buttermilk. It should always be mixed with other dry ingredients before the liquid is added.

Yeast is a single-cell organism that converts the natural sugars in flour to produce carbon dioxide. Yeast needs warmth, moisture, and food (sugars) to work. It is available in both dried and fresh forms for baking.

Greasing & Lining Pans

For many simple yellow cakes, you just need to give the bottom and sides of the pan a quick brush of oil or melted butter and insert a piece of nonstick parchment paper in the bottom. Richer or low-fat batters usually need a thoroughly greased and lined pan to prevent sticking.

Lining a Round Pan

1 Grease the pan. Cut a strip of parchment paper about 1 inch/2.5 cm longer than the circumference and about 1 inch/2.5 cm deeper than the pan.

2 Fold up one long edge about ½ inch/1 cm, then unfold, leaving a crease.

3 Use scissors to snip cuts along the folded edge of the paper so that it can be eased into the pan to fit around the curve at the bottom.

4 Place the pan on a sheet of parchment paper and draw around it with a pencil to mark the size. Cut with scissors just inside the line, making a round to fit inside the bottom, covering the snipped edges of the side lining paper. Grease the paper.

Lining a Square Pan

1 Grease the pan. Cut a strip of parchment paper about 1 inch/2.5 cm longer than the circumference of the pan and 1 inch/2.5 cm deeper.

2 Fold up one long edge about ½ inch/1 cm, then unfold, leaving a crease. Fit the paper into the sides of the pan, cutting a diagonal slit into the folded edge to fit each corner.

3 Place the pan on a sheet of parchment paper, draw around it to mark the size, then cut just inside the line to make a square. Lay the square inside the pan, covering the folded edges. Grease the paper.

Lining a Jelly Roll Pan and Sheet Pan

1 Grease the bottom and sides of the pan. Cut a piece of parchment paper 2¾ inches/7 cm larger than the pan.

2 Place the pan on the paper, then make a cut from each corner of the paper in toward the pan corner.

3 Place the paper inside the pan so that the diagonally cut corners overlap and fit neatly. Grease the paper.

Lining a Loaf Pan

1 Grease the pan. Cut a strip of parchment paper the length of the pan bottom and wide enough to cover the bottom and long sides. Place the paper in the pan.

2 Cut a second piece of parchment paper the width of the pan bottom and long enough to cover the bottom and ends of the pan. Slot this in over the first piece to line the pan, then grease the paper.

Flouring Pans

1 Grease the bottom and sides of the pan, then slip a piece of parchment paper in the bottom. Grease the paper.

2 Sprinkle a little flour into the pan. Tilt the pan, tapping lightly so the flour coats the bottom and sides evenly. Tip out any excess.

Essential Recipes: Cakes

The main ingredients for making cakes are flour, fat, sugar, and eggs. The proportion of fat to flour will influence the method by which the cake is made. With half or less fat to flour, the rubbing-in method is used, while with half or more fat to flour, the creaming method is used. If little or no fat is used, then whisking is the appropriate method.

Creamed Cakes

The most well-known of cakes made by this method is the yellow cake, which uses butter, sugar, eggs, and flour in equal quantities to make a light and airy cake. It makes a good base for many variations. Cakes made by this method should have a light, even texture. The higher the proportion of fat, sugar, and eggs to flour, the richer the cake will be.

Storage Cakes made by the creaming method keep well in an airtight container. Undecorated cakes freeze well.

All-In-One Cakes

This is a simplified variation of the creaming method. All the ingredients are beaten together at once until smooth. Extra baking powder helps to make the cake rise and soft margarine or butter is essential for it to mix fully. This gives a close-textured cake and is an ideal method when you are short of time.

Whisked Yellow Cakes

Whisked cakes depend on the amount of air trapped into the eggs and sugar during the whisking of the eggs. The eggs should be at room temperature. The best results are achieved by using an electric mixer.

Storage Fat-free cakes are best eaten on the day they are made. Those with some fat will keep a little longer if stored in an airtight container.

Rubbed-In Cakes

This method of cake mixing produces a plain, coarse texture and is often used for breads and cookies. The proportion of fat to flour varies from 25 percent to 50 percent. Rubbing in the fat with the fingertips held high over the bowl incorporates air. Liquid is added and the mixture is then gently brought together. Be careful not to overwork the batter or the results will be tough.

Storage Rubbed-in cakes, such as biscuits, should be kept for no more than three days, because they tend to become dry over time.

Melted Cakes

A few dense, moist cakes, such as gingerbread, employ this method. The fat and sugar are melted together before the dry ingredients are stirred in.

Storage These cakes are best if left for one day before eating to become moist. They keep well in an airtight container.

Creamed Cakes

All-In-One Cakes

Whisked Yellow Cakes

Small Cakes

The same basic principles and techniques for making large cakes also apply to small cakes. However, the oven temperature is usually higher and the baking time much shorter. Small cakes, each not much more than a couple of bites in size, can be cooked in a 12-hole mini muffin pan. For more substantial individual cakes, a muffin pan can be used. Lining the pans with paper liners will ensure that they turn out easily. Some small cakes are made as one large cake and then cut into appropriately sized bars or squares. This is a quick way of producing individual cakes. Small cakes should be simply decorated or left plain.

Curdling In Cake Batter

Curdling is the term used when the water from the eggs separates out from the fat globules in the cake batter, and is usually caused by the eggs being too cold. A curdled cake batter will hold less air and will produce a cake with a dense texture. To help prevent curdling, use eggs at room temperature. If your batter does begin to curdle, beat in a tablespoon of the flour to help bind the mixture back together. This is not a true curdling, which is the process of separating the curds from the whey in milk.

Is It Cooked?

Follow the timings in the recipe as a guideline, but also rely on your own judgment, because ovens vary in temperature. Small cakes should be well risen, firm, and springy to the touch, and yellow cakes should also be springy to the touch.

Test by gently pressing the cake with a finger. Once you have removed your finger, the cake should spring back, but if you can still see the fingerprint, return the cake to the oven for a few minutes longer. Fruitcake and deep yellow cakes are best tested with a toothpick inserted into the center. The toothpick will come out clean when the cake is cooked.

For most cakes, let cool for a few minutes in the pan before turning out and transferring to a wire rack to cool completely. Some cakes, such as rich fruitcakes, benefit from being left to cool completely in the pan—the recipe will specify this where necessary.

Rubbed-In Cakes

Melted Cakes

Small Cakes

Essential Recipes: Pastry

Basic pie dough and pastries are not as difficult to make as is sometimes perceived. Although preparing other, more special pastries is an area of baking that does require a certain amount of skill, by following the recipes closely, that skill can be acquired and professional results achieved with a little practice.

Cooking Pastry and Pie Dough

The oven must be hot when the pastry is first put in so that it will rise when the air that it contains is heated. The gluten in the flour absorbs the water and stretches and entangles the air in the dough as the air expands. The heat of the oven then sets the pastry in its risen shape. As it cooks, the starch grains in the flour will also burst and absorb the fat. If the oven is too cool, the fat will melt and run out while the flour remains uncooked, resulting in a heavy, soggy, and greasy pastry. After the pastry is set, the temperature can be reduced to cook the filling, if required.

Types of Pastry

All kinds of pastry, except crust, use all-purpose flour. Whole wheat flour can be used instead of all-purpose, but it produces heavier results and requires extra liquid to bring it together.

Flaky Pie Dough

Perhaps the most common home-baked pastry, this is also one of the easiest to master as long as the basic rules of pastry making are followed. A proportion of half fat to flour is used.

1 cup all-purpose flour
½ cup unsalted butter
2–3 tbsp cold water

Basic Method

1 Sift the flour into a bowl.

2 Cut the fat into small cubes and add to the flour. Rub in using your fingertips, lifting your hand high above the bowl to incorporate more air. The mixture will resemble fine breadcrumbs when the fat has been fully rubbed in.

3 Stir in any additional flavorings, if using, such as ground nuts, cheese, or sugar, for sweet pastry.

4 Add the liquid all at once and use your fingers to bring the dough together. Turn the dough out onto a lightly floured surface and knead very lightly. Ideally, the dough should be wrapped in foil or plastic wrap and chilled in the refrigerator for 30 minutes to let the dough "relax," which helps to prevent it from shrinking when it is baked.

5 Roll out the dough on a lightly floured surface. Rolling should be carried out in short, sharp strokes, with a light, even pressure in a forward movement only. Turn the dough as you roll.

6 Use as required, then let the dough relax again in a cool place for 15–30 minutes before baking. This is especially important if you have not previously relaxed the dough.

7 Bake in a hot oven for 15–20 minutes, until set. The temperature may then be reduced.

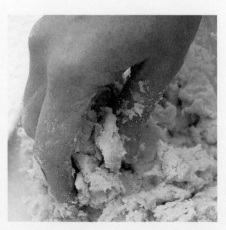

Baking Blind

When used to line a pan, flaky pie dough is often precooked to set the dough before the filling is added. The term used to describe this is "baking blind."

1 Line the pan with the rolled-out dough and prick the bottom with a fork.

2 Chill for about 30 minutes in the refrigerator or 10 minutes in the freezer (you can also bake pastry shells blind from frozen).

3 Line the pastry shell with a sheet of nonstick parchment paper, wax paper, or foil and fill with purpose-made ceramic or metal pie weights or use dried beans or rice. These weights help to conduct heat and cook the dough, as well as preventing the dough from puffing up in the center.

4 Bake for 10 minutes, then remove the paper and weights and bake for an additional 10 minutes, until the pastry is just golden.

5 Remove from the oven and brush a little beaten egg or egg white over the bottom to seal (the heat of the pastry shell will cook the egg).

Cook's Tip

It is important to follow a few basic rules when making pastry. Always measure the ingredients accurately and keep everything cool. Always use a light touch and handle the pastry with care. Knead the dough just sufficiently to bind it together—overkneading will start to develop the gluten in the flour and result in a tough, greasy pastry. Roll out pastry lightly, being careful not to stretch it unduly. Use only a small amount of flour when rolling out to avoid upsetting the careful balance of ingredients. Let the pastry rest in the refrigerator, wrapped in foil or plastic wrap, before rolling. A little salt may be added to bring out the flavor of pastry, but if salted butter or margarine is used, this is usually unnecessary.

Puff Pastry

Both puff pastry and filo dough are more difficult to make and very time consuming, but their richness, especially in the case of puff pastry, gives them a superior flavor. More experienced bakers will enjoy the challenge of making these pastries as well as the end results. The principle behind the pastry is to create many layers of dough and butter by folding and turning the two together. For an evenly layered pastry, it is important that you always roll it to the same thickness and that the edges are very straight and even.

scant 2½ cups all-purpose flour
¾ cup unsalted butter
½ cup cold water

Basic Method

1 Sift the flour into a bowl and rub in one-quarter of the butter.

2 Add the water and use your fingers to bring the dough together. Knead briefly to form a smooth dough. Put in a plastic bag and chill in the refrigerator for 30 minutes.

3 Roll out the remaining butter between two sheets of plastic wrap to form a block about ½ inch/1 cm thick.

4 Roll out the dough to a square about four times the size of the block of butter.

5 Put the block of butter in the center of the dough and fold over the corners of the dough to completely enclose the butter.

6 Roll out the dough into a rectangle three times as long as it is wide.

7 Fold one-third of the dough over to cover the middle third, then fold the remainder over the top.

8 Give the dough a half turn, roll out to form another rectangle, and fold again as before. Repeat the initial rolling and folding six times in total, chilling the dough frequently between rolling.

9 Let relax for a final 30 minutes, then use as required. Trim the folded edges of the dough before using to assist the rising. Bake in a hot oven. The pastry should rise 6–8 times its original height.

Filo Dough

It is advisable to use a white bread flour or all-purpose flour for filo dough. After the initial fat has been added, the dough is kneaded to develop the elasticity of the gluten, resulting in an elastic dough that will rise easily. A little lemon juice could be added to help develop the gluten and counteract the richness of the pastry. The dough must be left to relax before being baked. Once cooked, the filo dough does not keep long unless frozen, although the uncooked dough can be stored in the refrigerator for up to 48 hours. Uncooked dough can also be sealed and frozen for up to four months.

heaping 1½ cups all-purpose flour
¾ cup unsalted butter
6–7 tbsp cold milk or water

Basic Method

1 Sift the flour into a bowl and rub in one-quarter of the fat.

2 Add the water and use your fingers to bring the mixture together. Knead briefly to form a smooth dough.

3 Roll out the dough into a rectangle three times as long as it is wide.

4 Dot one-third of the remaining fat over two-thirds of the dough in rough lumps. Fold the uncovered dough over to cover half the fatted dough, then fold the remaining third over the top.

5 Seal the edges of the dough by pressing down with a rolling pin.

6 Give the dough a half turn, roll out to form another rectangle, and repeat steps 4 and 5 twice more until all the fat has been used. Put the dough in a plastic bag and chill in the refrigerator for 30 minutes.

7 Roll and fold the dough three more times as before, but without the addition of fat. Let relax for a final 30 minutes, then use as required. Trim the folded edges of the dough before using to assist the rising. Bake in a hot oven.

Rough Puff

This pastry is relatively easy to make and produces a fabulous light, flaky pastry. It can be a little sticky to handle to begin with. It has a similar fat content to filo dough.

heaping 1½ cups all-purpose flour
¾ cup unsalted butter
6–7 tbsp cold milk or water

Basic Method

1 Sift the flour into a bowl and add the fat cut into small squares or lumps.

2 Add the water and use your fingers to bring the dough together. Knead very lightly.

3 Roll and fold the dough as for puff pastry.

Crust Pastry

Crust pastry is a filling, homely kind of pastry. You can use either self-rising flour or all-purpose flour, but if you use all-purpose flour also use the baking powder and salt.

heaping 1½ cups self-rising or all-purpose flour
¾ cup lard or vegetable shortening
2¼ tsp baking powder (optional)
¾ tsp salt (optional)
⅔ cup cold water

Basic Method

1 Sift the flour into a bowl.

2 Mix the lard into the flour along with the baking powder and salt, if using.

3 Add enough water to form an elastic dough.

4 Only roll out the dough once to avoid producing a hard pastry.

Hot Watercrust Pastry

This traditional type of pastry is used for raised pies, such as pork or game pies. It is the exception to one of the basic rules of pastry making in that its success depends on the warmth of the utensils and flour throughout the making and shaping. If it becomes too cold, it will be difficult to handle.

scant 1 cup all-purpose flour
heaping ⅓ cup vegetable shortening
5 tbsp water

Basic Method

1 Sift the flour into a bowl and make a well in the center.

2 Put the shortening and water in a pan and heat until the fat melts, then bring to a boil. Immediately add to the well in the flour and mix with a spoon to form a dough, then knead the dough.

3 The dough should be shaped while still warm and cooked in a hot oven.

Choux Pastry

This is a rich, soft pastry that relies predominately on its high-water content, which becomes very hot during cooking to form a hollow pastry shell.

heaping ½ cup white bread flour
4 tbsp unsalted butter
⅔ cup water
2 eggs

Basic Method

1 Sift the flour.

2 Put the butter and water in a pan and heat until the fat melts.

3 Add the flour to the pan all at once and beat with a wooden spoon until the mixture forms a ball around the spoon. Let cool slightly.

4 Gradually beat in the eggs until the dough is smooth and glossy. The more the mixture is beaten, the better the results, because more air is incorporated.

5 Shape by piping or with a spoon, as required. Bake in a hot oven.

Covering a Pie

This is the basic method for making a single crust to cover a savory or sweet pie filling. You can then add decorative details and a glaze to enhance the appearance of the pie.

1 Roll out the pie dough to about 2 inches/5 cm larger all around the top of the dish.

2 Cut a strip about 1 inch/2.5 cm wide from the edge of the dough.

3 Moisten the edge of the dish and stick the dough strip to the dish.

4 Fill the pie and dampen the dough strip with a little water.

5 Using a rolling pin, carefully lift the dough over the pie. Press the edge down to seal.

6 Using a sharp knife, trim the edge and make a small hole in the center of the pie to let the steam escape.

Pastry Finishes

You can finish the pastry in several ways:

• Use a blunt knife to tap the edge of the pie and raise it. This also helps to seal the pie fully.
• Press the edge with a floured fork.
• Press one thumb around the edge while you pinch the outside edge between your other thumb and index finger.
• Press a thumb around the edge and draw a knife in a short distance from the edge toward the center of the pie between each thumbprint to create a scalloped edge.
• Decorate the pie by using the pastry trimmings. Cut them into leaves or other shapes, as desired, and stick to the pie crust by moistening slightly.

Glazes

Glazing the dough will produce a shiny golden surface once baked. You can use milk, beaten egg mixed with a little water, or lightly beaten egg white for glazing. Brush a thin layer over the dough with a pastry brush, but avoid making the dough too wet. For sweet pies, a little superfine sugar can also be sprinkled on top.

Essential Recipes: Cookies

From the flat, thin wafer to the traditionally chunky chocolate chip cookie, you can find a cookie that is perfect for just about any occasion, be it a decadent coffee morning, hearty afternoon tea, an elegant dinner, or a packed lunch on the run. As might be guessed from the numerous styles of cookies, there are several methods for preparing them.

Because cookies cook quickly, you will need to keep a close eye on the baking until you become more experienced in gauging the exact cooking time easily. For most cookies, let cool on the cookie sheet for a few minutes before transferring to a wire rack to cool completely. Many cookies are very soft when they come out of the oven but become crisp on cooling, so remember to remove them from the sheet before they become completely cold or they may stick. Store in an airtight container to retain freshness and crispness. Most cookies also freeze well—simply thaw at room temperature.

Rolled and Molded Cookies

Here the cookie dough is rolled out and cut out or shaped into logs, balls, or crescents. Be careful not to add too much extra flour when rolling and shaping, because this will alter the careful balance of the ingredients. If a dough is very soft, you may find it easier to roll out between two sheets of plastic wrap. Try to avoid rerolling too many times, or the cookies may become tough.

Drop Cookies

These are the quickest and easiest to make. They are often made by the creaming method, where the fat and sugar are beaten together, then the flour and any additional flavorings, such as nuts or chocolate chips, are added. The mixture is then beaten just enough to bring all the ingredients together in a soft dough, which can then be dropped onto the cookie sheet from spoons. Always space the drops of dough well apart on the cookie sheet, because the cookies will spread during baking.

Piped Cookies

Some cookies are piped from a plain or fluted pastry tip to produce a decorative effect. The consistency of the cookie dough needs to be just right—too stiff and the dough will be hard to pipe; too soft and the cookies will lose their shape when baked.

Wafers

Some classic cookies are very thin and crisp. The mixture is very soft (that of a batter) and is spooned onto a cookie sheet and spread out to form a circle. These are probably the hardest cookies to bake, because they bake very rapidly. They are sometimes shaped into rolls or curled. In this case, you need to work fast, only baking a couple at a time, because they need to be shaped while still warm.

Sliced Cookies

The dough in this instance is firm and can be shaped into a log. The individual cookies are then sliced at the desired thickness. The uncooked cookie dough can be stored in the refrigerator for several days and a few cookies cut and baked from the log as desired. This is an ideal way of making freshly baked cookies every day.

Essential Recipes: Breads & Yeast

There are so many different kinds of homemade bread that they can easily fill a book in themselves. Many, such as soda bread, plain white bread, malt bread, and rolls, are great basics, but once mastered, the temptation to move on to making delicious flavored breads is hard to resist. Not all breads rely on yeast as a leavening agent and you will find a selection of breads made without yeast in this book.

Yeast cooking is not particularly difficult and the results are most rewarding. In contrast to working with pie dough, a warm kitchen will help you on the way. Also, there is no need for the caution in handling that pie dough requires—a firm hand is perfect for kneading the dough to develop the gluten content of the bread, which gives it its unique texture. Of course, you do need to leave more time to produce yeasted products, but for the most part they can be left alone to rise while you are free to do other things. Most yeasted breads and bakes freeze well, so when time is plentiful, they are ideal for batch baking. The frozen bakes can be thawed at room temperature and refreshed in a hot oven for 5 minutes to warm through before serving.

Types of Yeast

Yeast is the leavening agent most frequently used for breads. It is a living organism that, when active, creates carbon dioxide. Small bubbles of carbon dioxide then become trapped within the structure of the dough, giving bread its characteristic structure.There are two main types of bread yeasts available: fresh and dry.

Fresh Yeast

This can be purchased from health food stores and some bakeries. It has a creamy color and is moist and firm. Fresh yeast is usually dissolved in liquid and left for a preliminary fermentation before being added to the remaining ingredients. It will only keep for a few days in the refrigerator, but can be frozen for up to three months.

Dry Yeast

This is available in two forms. Regular active dry yeast requires a preliminary fermentation and is activated by mixing with a little liquid and sugar or flour. Instant yeast, quick yeast, and rapid-rise active dry yeast are just some of the different names for yeast that does not require this preliminary fermentation and is simply stirred into the flour before the liquid is added. The first rising and punching down can also be eliminated if time is short. Dry yeast has a longer shelf life than fresh yeast and does not need to be refrigerated.

Effects of Temperature on Yeast

Yeast works quickest in warm temperatures, so it is generally recommended that the dough is left in a warm place to rise. However, yeast does not stop working at lower temperatures—it simply slows down. Therefore, dough can be made, shaped, and then left to rise overnight in a refrigerator. Let the dough return to room temperature before baking. Yeast that is left to work in slower conditions produces a loaf that many people regard as having more flavor and character.

Effects of Other Ingredients on Yeast Action

A basic loaf consists of just flour, yeast, salt, and water, but some breads, as well as cakes and even pastries, are made with yeast doughs that have been enriched with other ingredients, such as butter, sugar, and eggs. Additional ingredients may contribute to the rising, give added color to the crumb and crust, and may also improve the keeping qualities. However, all these additional ingredients will have an effect on the action of yeast.

Sugar in small amounts speeds up the action of yeast, but in larger quantities—above ¼ cup per 3⅓ cups—it will retard the action of yeast.

Fat in proportions above 2 tablespoons per 3⅓ cups will retard the action of yeast.

Eggs, because of their fat content, may slow the action of yeast, but they also have the ability to retain air in the mixture, so often help to produce a lighter texture.

To overcome any adverse effects of these added ingredients:

• Leave additional time for the rising—2 hours or more is not unusual.
• Make the dough in two parts, with the additional ingredients added after an initial rising.
• Extra yeast may be added.

Gluten

Gluten is formed by a combination of two proteins, gliadin and glutenin, which are found in wheat flour. Bread flours have a higher proportion of these proteins than normal flour. When these proteins are hydrated, they bond with each other, creating a large protein called gluten that gives the bread its structure. The longer the dough is kneaded, the stronger the gluten becomes and the better texture the bread has. It is possible to knead the dough so much that it becomes too warm and the gluten begins to break down, but this is very unlikely to happen if kneading by hand. If you choose to knead in a mixer, knead for short bursts, resting it a few seconds each time for the dough to cool slightly.

Yeast-Free Breads

Some breads do not contain yeast. These breads use another method to leaven the bread (make the bread rise) or are unleavened. Sometimes called quick breads, soda bread, and cornbread fall into the former category. Baking soda or baking powder is added to the dough. These produce carbon dioxide, a process that begins as soon as the dough is mixed, so the bread must be baked immediately. The dough should be soft and sticky, and in some cases is more like a thick batter. Quick breads have a soft, crumbly texture and some are best served warm. Most are best eaten the day they are made.

Unleavened breads are sometimes called flat breads. Some flat breads, such as naan and pita breads, are in fact leavened with yeast but unleavened dough can also be used. Flat breads are among the oldest breads. Evidence has been found that they were cooked on stones in Neolithic times. Paratha, tortillas, and chapatis are all examples of yeast-free flat breads. In the modern home, they can be cooked on a griddle or in a heavy-bottom skillet. Flat breads can be topped, such as pizza and focaccia, stuffed, such as pitta bread, filled with beans and rice and rolled, such as chapattis and tortillas, or used for dipping, such as poppadums from India.

Making Yeast Breads
Basic Method

The method used is basically the same for all yeast breads, although individual steps may vary according to the recipe.

4¾ cups white bread flour
2 tsp salt
2 tsp active dry yeast
2 tbsp olive oil or butter
about 2 cups lukewarm water

1 Sift the flour and salt into a large bowl. Stir in the active dry yeast, and make a well in the center. Pour in the liquids and mix to a soft, slightly sticky dough.

2 Turn out the dough onto a lightly floured surface and begin kneading by folding the dough over on top of itself and pushing away with the palm of your hand—do not be afraid to be forceful. Keep kneading, giving the dough a quarter turn as you do so, for 10 minutes, or until the dough is very smooth and elastic and no longer sticky. Alternatively, knead the dough in an electric mixer fitted with a dough hook for 6–8 minutes.

3 Form the dough into a ball and put in a lightly oiled bowl. Rub a little oil over the surface of the dough to prevent it from drying out, and cover loosely with plastic wrap or slide the bowl inside a clean

polythene bag. Let rise in a warm place for 1 hour, or until doubled in size.

4 When the dough has increased to double its original size, turn out onto a lightly floured surface and lightly knead again for a few minutes. This is called "punching down," because some of the air that has been incorporated into the dough is punched out and the dough shrinks in size. This ensures that the bread has a more even texture, because any large air pockets are removed at this stage.

5 Shape the dough as required and place in a lightly greased loaf pan. The dough should fill the pan halfway.

6 Cover loosely again and let rise for a second time until doubled in size.

7 Bake in a preheated hot oven. To test if the bread is cooked, turn out of the pan and tap the bottom. The loaf should sound hollow. Let cool on a wire rack.

Bread Machines

You can make bread with the minimum of fuss and effort by using a bread machine. Once all the ingredients have been measured and added to the pan, the machine can be left to do the hard work and a few hours later you have a freshly baked loaf. Although some of the fun of making bread is removed, it is nevertheless a very convenient way of producing freshly baked, warm bread, and because most machines have a timer, you can set it so that you can enjoy it when you wake up in the morning. Always follow the manufacturer's instructions, because quantities of ingredients and methods may vary.

A Note About Salt

Salt is an essential ingredient in bread making, because it not only adds flavor but also strengthens the gluten structure, and helps control the growth of yeast. Too little and the result will be a poor gluten structure; too much and the salt will inhibit the action of the yeast. Both will result in a loaf of poor volume and flavor. For this reason, it is important not to vary the amount of salt in a recipe, even if you are trying to reduce your salt intake, because this will adversely affect the finished product.

Top Hints for Successful Baking

Before You Start

- Always preheat the oven to the correct temperature so it's ready to use when your cake is mixed. Leave at least 10 minutes for preheating.
- Grease pans lightly with a mild-flavored oil, such as sunflower oil, or melted butter. Use a pastry brush to cover the pan quickly and evenly.
- For creamed mixtures, such as layer cakes, line the bottom of the pan with nonstick parchment paper; for rich mixtures and fruitcakes, line the bottom and sides of the pan. For very rich fruitcakes, wrap a double thickness of brown paper around the outside of the pan for extra protection and tie with string to secure.
- If you don't have the correct-size pan for the recipe, or prefer to use an unusual shape pan, such as a heart-shape pan, just match the capacity—for example, an 8-inch/20-cm round pan holds the same volume of liquid as a 7-inch/18-cm square pan.
- Assemble all your ingredients and measure everything before you start to mix.

The Perfect Mix

- Always sift the flour with leavening agents or spices before adding to a mixture so that they are evenly distributed throughout the mix.
- If you run out of self-rising flour, add 1½ teaspoons of baking powder plus ½ teaspoon of salt to every 1 cup all-purpose flour and sift together thoroughly before use.
- Most cake recipes use either butter or hard (block) margarine, which are interchangeable although butter has a much better flavor. Soft (tub) margarines and oil are good for all-in-one recipes, but less successful for creamed methods. Low-fat spreads have a high-water content and give poor results in conventional recipes.
- For most recipes, fats should be used at room temperature for ease of mixing. Hard butter or block margarine can be softened for a few seconds in the microwave to make mixing easier.
- It's best to use eggs at room temperature for baking because they give a better volume and hold more air when whisked. If you usually store your eggs in the refrigerator, remove them about 30 minutes before you start to mix.
- To separate eggs, tap the shell against the side of a mixing bowl to crack, then break open, letting the white run out into the bowl and holding the yolk in one half of the shell. Tip the yolk backward and forward from shell to shell to let all the white run into the bowl.
- When folding in flour, use a metal spoon, cutting through the mixture with a light, quick action to keep as much air in it as possible. Overmixing can result in a heavy, close-textured cake.

Baked to Perfection

- Unless otherwise stated, place your cake on the center shelf of the oven to bake. If your oven tends to cook more quickly at the back or sides, carefully turn the cake pan or cookie sheet around toward the end of the cooking time.
- Resist the temptation to open the oven door too often during cooking, and close it gently rather than banging it shut. It's best to try to wait until at least halfway through the cooking time before sneaking a look. A quick peep won't harm the cake, but if you open the door too often, the temperature will drop and this may prevent the cake from rising properly.
- To test light yellow cakes for doneness, press the top lightly with a fingertip—the cake should feel spongy to the touch and spring back when released. To check rich fruitcakes for doneness, listen closely—if the cake is still sizzling inside, it is not yet thoroughly cooked. Most large cakes will shrink slightly from the sides of the pan when they are cooked. As a final test, insert a toothpick or skewer into the center of the cake, then lift it out. If the cake is cooked, it should come out clean; if it's sticky, the mixture needs more cooking.
- Most cakes should be cooled slightly in the pan before turning out, because they shrink from the sides of the pan and become firmer, so turning out is easier.
- Use a metal wire rack for cooling cakes to make sure that any excess steam can escape without making the cake soggy. If you don't have a wire rack, use the rack from a broiler pan or a barbecue rack.
- Always make sure your cake is completely cool before storing, because if any steam remains, it can cause mold.

Glossary of Baking Terms

Baking Blind

Baking a pastry shell without filling. Place a round of parchment paper or wax paper in the pastry shell and fill with dried beans, rice, or ceramic pie weights, then bake as the recipe instructs.

Beating

A method of vigorously agitating with a spoon, fork, or electric mixer to combine ingredients evenly, to soften ingredients, such as butter, or to incorporate air into mixtures.

Creaming

To beat together mixtures of fat and sugar to soften to a pale, fluffy consistency, incorporating air into the mix to make a light, spongy cake, such as a layer cake.

Dredging

To sprinkle a mixture or surface generously with a dry ingredient, such as flour or confectioners' sugar, either using a sifter or a dredger, which has a top with holes for even sprinkling.

Dusting

To sprinkle a surface lightly with a dry ingredient, such as flour, confectioners' sugar, or spices, to give a thin coating, using a fine sifter or dredger to distribute evenly.

Folding In

A method of combining a creamed mixture with dry ingredients, or to incorporate whisked egg whites, so that as little air as possible is knocked out. Ideally, use a large metal spoon to cut and fold the dry ingredients through the mixture, agitating as little as possible to retain air bubbles for lightness.

Glazing

To brush a coating over a mixture, either before or after baking, to give a glossy appearance or improve the flavor. For instance, beaten egg or milk are used to glaze pastries and breads, and syrups or jellies may be brushed over a cake top for an attractive finish.

Kneading

A process of pressing and stretching a dough, with the hands or a dough hook, to strengthen the gluten (the protein in wheat flour). This makes the gluten more elastic, enabling the dough to rise easily and giving an even texture to the finished product.

Punching Down

This is a second kneading, usually done after the dough has been left to rise and before shaping, with the purpose of punching out any large air bubbles from the dough to guarantee an even-textured result.

Piping

Forcing a soft cake or cookie mixture, or a frosting, from a pastry bag through a tip, usually to create a decorative shape or effect, such as stars, rosettes, or lines. Use a firm, even pressure for best results.

Rising

To let a bread dough stand after shaping, usually in a warm place. This is done to let the dough rise and give the finished bread a good rise and a light, even texture.

Rubbing In

A method of incorporating fat, such as butter, into dry ingredients, such as flour, using the fingertips to rub the two together evenly. The fingertips are the coolest part of the hand, and a cool, light touch helps to give a short texture to pie dough, cookies, and cakes.

Sifting

To shake dry ingredients, such as flour, through a sifter or strainer to eliminate lumps and create a smooth texture. It can also help to evenly distribute any added leavening agents or spices.

Whipping

A term used to describe the gentle beating of a mixture, usually with a mixer, to make it smooth or incorporate air. For example, it is used to thicken heavy cream, or make it stiff enough for piping.

Whisking

Rapidly beating a mixture using a hand whisk or electric mixer to incorporate and trap large amounts of air. This method is used for whisked yellow cakes, which rely totally on air for a light, open texture, and meringues, where egg whites are whisked until they are stiff enough to hold peaks.

Chapter 1
Cakes

Yellow Layer Cake

Serves 8–10

ingredients

- ¾ cup unsalted butter, softened, plus extra for greasing
- ¾ cup superfine sugar
- 3 eggs, beaten
- scant 1½ cups self-rising flour
- pinch of salt
- 3 tbsp raspberry jelly
- 1 tbsp superfine or confectioners' sugar

1 Preheat the oven to 350°F/180°C. Grease two 8-inch/20-cm round cake pans and line with wax or parchment paper.

2 Cream the butter and superfine sugar together in a mixing bowl using a wooden spoon or an electric mixer, until the batter is pale in color and light and fluffy.

3 Add the eggs, one at a time, beating well after each addition. Sift the flour and salt together into a separate bowl and carefully add to the batter, folding it in with a metal spoon or a spatula. Divide the batter between the pans and smooth over with a spatula.

4 Place the pans in the center of the preheated oven and bake for 25–30 minutes, until well risen, golden brown, and beginning to shrink from the sides of the pan.

5 Remove from the oven and let stand for 1 minute. Loosen the cakes from around the edge of the pans using a palette knife. Turn the cakes out onto a clean dish towel, remove the paper, and invert the cakes onto a wire rack (this prevents the wire rack from marking the top of the cakes).

6 When completely cool, sandwich together the cakes with the jelly and sprinkle with the superfine or confectioners' sugar.

Orange & Poppy Seed
Bundt Cake

Serves 10

ingredients

- scant 1 cup unsalted butter, plus extra for greasing
- 1 cup superfine sugar
- 3 extra large eggs, beaten
- finely grated rind of 1 orange
- ¼ cup poppy seeds
- 2¼ cups all-purpose flour, plus extra for dusting
- 2 tsp baking powder
- ⅔ cup milk
- ½ cup orange juice
- strips of orange zest, to decorate

syrup

- scant ¾ cup superfine sugar
- ⅔ cup orange juice

1 Preheat the oven to 325°F/160°C. Grease and lightly flour a 9-cup Bundt tube pan, about 9½ inches/24 cm in diameter.

2 Cream together the butter and sugar until pale and fluffy, then add the eggs gradually, beating thoroughly after each addition. Stir in the orange rind and poppy seeds. Sift in the flour and baking powder, then fold in evenly.

3 Add the milk and orange juice, stirring to mix evenly. Spoon the batter into the prepared pan and bake in the preheated oven for 45–50 minutes, or until firm and golden brown. Cool in the pan for 10 minutes, then turn out onto a wire rack to cool.

4 For the syrup, place the sugar and orange juice in a saucepan and heat gently until the sugar melts. Bring to a boil and simmer for about 5 minutes, until reduced and syrupy.

5 Spoon the syrup over the cake while it is still warm. Top with the strips of orange zest and serve warm or cold.

Double Chocolate Mint
Cake

Serves 8

ingredients

- heaping 1¼ cups all-purpose flour
- 2 tbsp unsweetened cocoa
- 1 tbsp baking powder
- ¾ cup unsalted butter, softened, plus extra for greasing
- scant 1 cup superfine sugar
- 3 eggs, beaten
- 1 tbsp milk
- 12 chocolate mint sticks, chopped, plus extra sticks to decorate
- ⅔ cup chocolate spread, plus extra to drizzle

1 Preheat the oven to 350°F/180°C. Grease two 8-inch/20-cm round cake pans and line with parchment paper.

2 Sift the flour, unsweetened cocoa, and baking powder together into a bowl and beat in the butter, sugar, and eggs, mixing until smooth. Stir in the milk and chocolate mint pieces.

3 Spread the batter into the prepared pans. Bake in the preheated oven for 25–30 minutes, until risen and firm. Let cool in the pans for 2 minutes, then turn out to cool on a wire rack.

4 Sandwich the cakes together with the chocolate spread, then drizzle more chocolate spread over the top. Decorate the cake with chocolate mint sticks.

Chocolate Fudge Cake

Serves 8

ingredients
- ¾ cup butter, softened, plus extra for greasing
- heaping 1 cup superfine sugar
- 3 eggs, beaten
- 3 tbsp light corn syrup
- 3 tbsp ground almonds
- heaping 1 cup self-rising flour
- pinch of salt
- ¼ cup unsweetened cocoa

frosting
- 8 oz/225 g semisweet chocolate, broken into pieces
- ¼ cup dark brown sugar
- 1 cup butter, diced
- 5 tbsp evaporated milk
- ¼ tsp vanilla extract

1 Grease two 8-inch/20-cm round cake pans and line with parchment paper.

2 To make the frosting, place the chocolate, brown sugar, butter, evaporated milk, and vanilla extract in a heavy-bottom pan. Heat gently, stirring continuously, until melted. Pour into a bowl and let cool. Cover and let chill in the refrigerator for 1 hour, or until spreadable.

3 Preheat the oven to 350°F/180°C. Place the butter and superfine sugar in a bowl and beat together until light and fluffy. Gradually beat in the eggs. Stir in the corn syrup and ground almonds. Sift the flour, salt, and cocoa into a separate bowl, then fold into the cake batter. Add a little water, if necessary, to make a dropping consistency.

4 Spoon the cake batter into the prepared pans and bake in the preheated oven for 30–35 minutes, or until springy to the touch and a toothpick inserted in the center comes out clean.

5 Let stand in the pans for 5 minutes, then turn out onto wire racks to cool completely. When the cakes have cooled, sandwich them together with half of the frosting. Spread the remaining frosting over the top and sides of the cake, swirling it to give a frosted appearance.

Coconut & Lime Cake

Serves 8

ingredients

- ¾ cup unsalted butter, softened, plus extra for greasing
- heaping ¾ cup superfine sugar
- 3 eggs, beaten
- 1 cup self-rising flour
- scant 1 cup unsweetened dried shredded coconut, plus ¼ cup, lightly toasted, for decorating
- grated rind and juice of 1 lime

icing

- 1½ cups confectioners' sugar
- grated rind and juice of 1 lime

1 Preheat the oven to 325°F/160°C. Grease an 8-inch/20-cm round cake pan and line with parchment paper.

2 Place the butter and sugar in a large bowl and beat together until pale and fluffy. Gradually beat in the eggs. Sift in the flour and gently fold in using a metal spoon. Fold in the coconut and the lime rind and juice.

3 Spoon the batter into the prepared pan and level the surface. Bake in the preheated oven for 1 hour–1 hour 10 minutes, until risen, golden, and firm to the touch. Let cool in the pan for 5 minutes, then turn out to cool completely on a wire rack.

4 For the icing, sift the confectioners' sugar into a bowl. Stir in the lime rind and juice to make a thick, smooth icing, adding a few drops of water, if necessary. Spoon the icing over the top of the cake, letting it drizzle down the sides of the cake. Scatter the toasted shredded coconut over the icing and let set.

Orange Cake

Serves 8

ingredients
- 2 oranges
- ¾ cup butter, softened, plus extra for greasing
- ¾ cup superfine sugar
- 3 eggs, lightly beaten
- 1¼ cups self-rising flour
- 3 tbsp ground almonds
- 3 tbsp light cream

glaze & topping
- 6 tbsp orange juice
- 2 tbsp superfine sugar
- 3 white sugar cubes, crushed

1 Preheat the oven to 350°F/180°C. Grease a 7-inch/18-cm round cake pan and line with parchment paper.

2 Pare the zest from the oranges and chop it finely. In a bowl, cream together the butter, sugar, and orange zest until pale and fluffy.

3 Gradually add the beaten eggs to the batter, beating thoroughly after each addition.

4 Gently fold in the flour, ground almonds, and light cream. Spoon the batter into the prepared pan.

5 Bake in the preheated oven for 55–60 minutes, or until a fine toothpick inserted into the center comes out clean. Let cool slightly.

6 Meanwhile, make the glaze. Put the orange juice into a small pan with the sugar. Bring to a boil over low heat and simmer for 5 minutes.

7 Turn out the cake onto a wire rack. Drizzle the glaze over the cake until it has been absorbed and sprinkle with the crushed sugar cubes. Let cool completely before serving.

Classic Cherry Cake

Serves 8

ingredients

- heaping 1 cup candied cherries, quartered
- ¾ cup ground almonds
- 1¾ cups all-purpose flour
- 1 tsp baking powder
- scant 1 cup butter, plus extra for greasing
- 3 sugar cubes, crushed, plus 6 sugar cubes, crushed, for sprinkling
- 3 extra large eggs
- finely grated rind and juice of 1 lemon

1 Preheat the oven to 350°F/180°C. Grease an 8-inch/20-cm round cake pan and line with parchment paper.

2 Stir together the candied cherries, ground almonds, and 1 tablespoon of the flour. Sift the remaining flour into a separate bowl with the baking powder.

3 Cream together the butter and sugar until light in color and fluffy in texture. Gradually add the eggs, beating hard with each addition, until evenly mixed.

4 Add the flour mixture and fold lightly and evenly into the creamed mixture with a metal spoon. Add the cherry mixture and fold in evenly. Finally, fold in the lemon rind and juice.

5 Spoon the batter into the prepared cake pan and sprinkle with the crushed sugar cubes. Bake in the preheated oven for 1–1¼ hours, or until risen, golden brown, and the cake is just beginning to shrink away from the sides of the pan.

6 Let cool in the pan for about 15 minutes, then turn out onto a wire rack to cool completely.

Spiced Apple & Raisin Cake

Serves 8–10

ingredients

- 1 cup unsalted butter, softened, plus extra for greasing
- heaping 1 cup light brown sugar
- 4 extra large eggs, lightly beaten
- scant 1⅔ cups self-rising flour
- 2 tsp ground cinnamon
- ½ tsp ground nutmeg
- ½ cup raisins
- 3 small apples, peeled, cored, and thinly sliced
- 2 tbsp honey, warmed

1 Preheat the oven to 350°F/180°C. Grease a 9-inch/23-cm round springform cake pan and line with parchment paper.

2 Place the butter and sugar in a large bowl and beat together until light and fluffy. Gradually beat in the eggs. Sift the flour, cinnamon, and nutmeg together into the batter and fold in gently using a metal spoon. Fold in the raisins.

3 Spoon half of the batter into the prepared pan and level the surface. Scatter over half of the sliced apples. Spoon over the rest of the cake mixture and gently level the surface. Arrange the rest of the apple slices over the top.

4 Bake in the preheated oven for 1 hour 10 minutes–1 hour 15 minutes, until risen, golden brown, and firm to the touch. Let cool in the pan for 10 minutes, then turn out onto a wire rack to cool. Brush the top with the warmed honey and let cool completely.

Gingerbread

Serves 12–16

ingredients

- 3¾ cups all-purpose flour
- 1 tbsp baking powder
- 1 tsp baking soda
- 1 tbsp ground ginger
- ¾ cup unsalted butter
- ¾ cup brown sugar
- ¾ cup dark molasses
- ¾ cup maple syrup or corn syrup
- 1 egg, beaten
- 1 cup milk

1 Preheat the oven to 325°F/160°C. Line a 9-inch/23-cm square cake pan, 2 inches/5 cm deep, with wax or parchment paper.

2 Sift the flour, baking powder, baking soda, and ground ginger together into a large mixing bowl.

3 Place the butter, sugar, molasses, and maple syrup in a medium saucepan and heat over low heat until the butter has melted and the sugar has dissolved. Set aside to cool briefly.

4 Mix the beaten egg with the milk and add to the cooled syrup mixture. Add the liquid ingredients to the dry ingredients and beat well using a wooden spoon until the batter is smooth and glossy.

5 Pour the batter into the prepared pan and bake in the center of the preheated oven for 1½ hours, until well risen and just firm to the touch. This makes a wonderful sticky gingerbread, but, if you like a firmer cake, cook for an additional 15 minutes.

6 Remove from the oven and let cool in the pan on a wire rack. When cooled, remove the cake from the pan with the wax paper. To store, wrap with foil and place in an airtight container for up to 1 week to let the flavors develop. Cut into wedges and serve.

Sticky Date Cake

Serves 6–8

ingredients
- scant ½ cup raisins
- heaping ¾ cup pitted dates, chopped
- 1 tsp baking soda
- 2 tbsp butter, plus extra for greasing
- 1 cup light brown sugar
- 2 eggs
- scant 1½ cups self-rising flour, sifted

sauce
- 2 tbsp butter
- ¾ cup heavy cream
- 1 cup light brown sugar

1 Preheat the oven to 350°F/180°C. Grease an 8-inch/20-cm round cake pan.

2 To make the cake, put the raisins, dates, and baking soda into a heatproof bowl. Cover with boiling water and set aside to soak. Put the butter in a separate bowl, add the sugar, and mix well. Beat in the eggs, then fold in the flour. Drain the soaked raisins and dates, add to the bowl, and mix.

3 Spoon the mixture evenly into the prepared pan. Bake in the preheated oven for 35–40 minutes, or until a toothpick inserted into the center comes out clean.

4 About 5 minutes before the end of the cooking time, make the sauce. Melt the butter in a pan over medium heat. Stir in the cream and sugar and bring to a boil, stirring constantly. Lower the heat and simmer for 5 minutes.

5 Turn the cake out onto a serving plate and let cool for 5 minutes. Cut into slices and serve on individual plates. Pour over the sauce and serve immediately.

Cornmeal & Almond Cake

Serves 6

ingredients

- scant 1 cup unsalted butter, softened, plus extra for greasing
- 1 cup superfine sugar
- juice and finely grated rind of 1 small orange
- 3 eggs, beaten
- 2¼ cups ground almonds
- 1⅔ cups instant cornmeal
- 1 tsp baking powder
- vanilla ice cream, to serve

1 Preheat the oven to 350°F/180°C. Grease a 9-inch/23-cm round cake pan and line with parchment paper.

2 Beat together the butter and sugar with an electric mixer until pale and fluffy.

3 Add the orange juice and rind, eggs, and almonds. Sift in the cornmeal and baking powder and beat until smooth.

4 Spread the mixture in the prepared pan, smoothing with a palette knife.

5 Bake in the preheated oven for 35–40 minutes, until firm and golden. Remove from the oven and let cool in the pan for 20 minutes.

6 Transfer the cake to a wire rack to cool. Cut the cake into slices and serve warm or cold with ice cream.

Spiced Sweet Loaf

Serves 10

ingredients

- ½ cup currants
- ⅓ cup raisins
- scant ¼ cup chopped candied peel
- ⅓ cup candied cherries, rinsed, dried, and quartered
- 2 tbsp dark rum
- 4 tbsp butter
- ¼ cup milk
- 3 tbsp superfine sugar
- 3¼ cups white bread flour, plus extra for dusting
- ½ tsp salt
- ½ tsp ground nutmeg
- ½ tsp ground cinnamon
- seeds from 3 cardamom pods
- 2 tsp active dry yeast
- finely grated rind of 1 lemon
- 1 egg, beaten
- ⅓ cup slivered almonds
- oil, for greasing
- 6 oz/175 g marzipan
- melted butter, for brushing
- confectioners' sugar, for dusting

1 Put the currants, raisins, candied peel, and candied cherries in a bowl. Stir in the rum and set aside. Put the butter, milk, and superfine sugar into a saucepan and heat gently until the sugar has dissolved and the butter has just melted. Let cool slightly.

2 Sift the flour, salt, nutmeg, and cinnamon into a bowl. Crush the cardamom seeds and add them to the flour mixture. Stir in the yeast. Make a well in the center and stir in the milk mixture, lemon rind, and egg. Beat to form a soft dough.

3 Turn out the dough onto a floured surface. With floured hands, knead the dough for about 5 minutes. It will be quite sticky, so add more flour if necessary. Knead the soaked fruit and slivered almonds into the dough until just combined.

4 Place the dough in a clean, lightly oiled bowl. Cover with plastic wrap and let stand in a warm place for 1½ hours, or until doubled in size. Turn out the dough onto a floured surface and knead lightly for 1–2 minutes, then roll out to a 10-inch/25-cm square.

5 Roll the marzipan into a sausage shape slightly shorter than the length of the dough and place down the center. Fold one side over to cover the marzipan. Repeat with the other side, overlapping in the center. Seal the ends. Place the roll, seam-side down, on a greased baking sheet. Cover with oiled plastic wrap and let stand in a warm place until doubled in size.

6 Preheat the oven to 375°F/190°C. Bake in the preheated oven for 40 minutes, or until it is golden and sounds hollow when tapped underneath. Brush the hot loaf generously with melted butter and dust heavily with confectioners' sugar. Let cool on a wire rack.

Chocolate & Almond
Layer Cake

Serves 10–12

ingredients
- 7 eggs
- 1¾ cups superfine sugar
- 1¼ cups all-purpose flour
- ¼ cup unsweetened cocoa
- 4 tbsp butter, melted,
  plus extra for greasing

filling
- 7 oz/200 g semisweet chocolate
- ½ cup butter
- 4 tbsp confectioners' sugar

to decorate
- ⅔ cup toasted slivered almonds,
  crushed lightly
- grated chocolate

1 Preheat the oven to 350°F/180°C. Grease a deep 9-inch/23-cm square cake pan and line with parchment paper.

2 Whisk the eggs and superfine sugar in a mixing bowl with an electric mixer for about 10 minutes, or until the batter is very light and foamy and the beaters leave a trail that lasts a few seconds when lifted.

3 Sift the flour and cocoa together and fold half into the batter. Drizzle over the melted butter and fold in the rest of the flour and cocoa. Pour into the prepared pan and bake in the preheated oven for 30–35 minutes, or until springy to the touch. Let cool slightly, then remove from the pan and cool completely on a wire rack.

4 To make the filling, melt the chocolate and butter together, then remove from the heat. Stir in the confectioners' sugar and let cool, then beat until thick enough to spread.

5 Halve the cake lengthwise and cut each half into three layers. Sandwich the layers together with three-quarters of the chocolate filling. Spread the remainder over the cake and mark a wavy pattern on the top. Press the almonds onto the sides. Decorate with grated chocolate.

Classic Carrot Cake

Serves 12

ingredients

- butter, for greasing
- 1 cup self-rising flour
- pinch of salt
- 1 tsp ground cinnamon
- ¾ cup light brown sugar
- 2 eggs
- scant ½ cup sunflower oil
- 2 medium carrots, peeled and finely grated
- ⅓ cup unsweetened dried shredded coconut
- ⅓ cup walnuts, chopped
- walnut pieces, for decorating

frosting

- 4 tbsp butter, softened
- 3 tbsp cream cheese
- 1½ cups confectioners' sugar, sifted
- 1 tsp lemon juice

1 Preheat the oven to 350°F/180°C. Grease an 8-inch/20-cm square cake pan and line with parchment paper.

2 Sift together the flour, salt, and ground cinnamon into a large bowl and stir in the brown sugar. Add the eggs and oil to the dry ingredients and mix well.

3 Stir in the grated carrot, shredded coconut, and chopped walnuts.

4 Pour the batter into the prepared pan and bake in the preheated oven for 20–25 minutes, or until just firm to the touch. Let cool in the pan.

5 Meanwhile, make the frosting. In a bowl, beat together the butter, cream cheese, confectioners' sugar, and lemon juice until the mixture is fluffy and creamy.

6 Turn the cake out of the pan and cut into 12 bars or slices. Spread with the frosting and then decorate with walnut pieces.

Banana Loaf

Serves 8

ingredients

- butter, for greasing
- scant 1 cup white self-rising flour
- scant ¾ cup whole wheat self-rising flour
- heaping ¾ cup raw brown sugar
- pinch of salt
- ½ tsp ground cinnamon
- ½ tsp ground nutmeg
- 2 large ripe bananas, peeled
- ¾ cup orange juice
- 2 eggs, beaten
- 4 tbsp canola oil

1 Preheat the oven to 350°F/180°C. Grease a 9 x 5 x 3¼-inch/23 x 13 x 8-cm loaf pan and line with parchment paper.

2 Sift the flours, sugar, salt, and the spices into a large bowl. In a separate bowl, mash the bananas with the orange juice, then stir in the eggs and oil. Pour into the dry ingredients and mix well.

3 Spoon into the prepared loaf pan and bake in the preheated oven for 1 hour, or until a toothpick inserted into the center comes out clean. If not, bake for an additional 10 minutes and test again.

4 Remove from the oven and let cool in the pan. Turn out onto a wire rack, slice, and serve.

Butternut Squash & Orange
Cake

Serves 10–12

ingredients
- ¾ cup butter, softened, plus extra for greasing
- ¾ cup light brown sugar
- 3 eggs, beaten
- finely grated rind and juice of 1 orange
- 2 cups whole wheat flour
- 3 tsp baking powder
- 1 tsp ground cinnamon
- 1⅓ cups coarsely grated butternut squash
- heaping ¾ cup raisins

topping
- 1 cup cream cheese
- ¼ cup confectioners' sugar, sifted
- thinly pared orange zest, to decorate

1 Preheat the oven to 350°F/180°C. Grease a deep 7-inch/18-cm round cake pan and line with parchment paper. For the cake, cream the butter and brown sugar together in a bowl until light and fluffy.

2 Gradually beat in the eggs, beating well after each addition. Reserve 1 teaspoon of the orange rind for the topping, then beat the remaining orange rind into the creamed mixture.

3 Fold in the flour, baking powder, and cinnamon, then fold in the squash, raisins, and a little orange juice, if necessary (about 1 tablespoon), to create a fairly soft consistency, reserving 2 – 3 teaspoons for the topping.

4 Spoon the batter into the prepared pan and level the surface. Bake in the preheated oven for about 1 hour, until risen, firm to the touch, and deep golden brown. Remove from the oven and cool in the pan for a few minutes, then turn out onto a wire rack. Remove the lining paper and let cool completely.

5 To make the topping, beat the cream cheese, confectioners' sugar, reserved grated orange rind, and 2–3 teaspoons of the reserved orange juice together in a bowl until smooth and combined. Spread over the top of the cold cake, swirling it attractively, then sprinkle with pared orange zest. Serve immediately in slices.

Lemon Cake

Serves 8

ingredients
- butter, for greasing
- 1¾ cups all-purpose flour
- 2 tsp baking powder
- 1 cup superfine sugar
- 4 eggs
- ⅔ cup sour cream
- grated rind of 1 large lemon
- 4 tbsp lemon juice
- ⅔ cup sunflower oil

syrup
- 4 tbsp confectioners' sugar
- 3 tbsp lemon juice

1 Preheat the oven to 350°F/180°C. Grease an 8-inch/20-cm loose-bottom, round cake pan and line with parchment paper.

2 Sift the flour and baking powder into a mixing bowl and stir in the superfine sugar.

3 In a separate bowl, whisk the eggs, sour cream, lemon rind, lemon juice, and oil together.

4 Pour the egg mixture into the dry ingredients and mix well until evenly combined.

5 Pour the batter into the prepared pan and bake in the preheated oven for 45–60 minutes, or until risen and golden brown.

6 Meanwhile, to make the syrup, mix together the confectioners' sugar and lemon juice in a small pan. Stir over low heat until just beginning to bubble and turn syrupy.

7 As soon as the cake comes out of the oven, prick the surface with a fine toothpick, then brush the syrup over the top. Let the cake cool completely in the pan before turning out and serving.

Double Chocolate Gâteau

Serves 10

ingredients
- 1 cup butter, softened, plus extra for greasing
- heaping 1 cup superfine sugar
- 4 eggs, beaten
- 1½ cups self-rising flour
- ½ cup unsweetened cocoa
- a little milk (optional)

filling
- generous 1 cup heavy cream
- 8 oz/225 g white chocolate, broken into pieces

frosting
- 12 oz/350 g semisweet chocolate, broken into pieces
- ½ cup butter
- scant ½ cup heavy cream

to decorate
- 4 oz/115 g semisweet chocolate curls
- 2 tsp confectioners' sugar and unsweetened cocoa, mixed

1 To make the filling, put the cream in a pan and heat to almost boiling. Put the white chocolate in a food processor and chop. With the motor running, pour the hot cream through the feed tube and process for 10–15 seconds, until smooth. Transfer to a bowl and let cool, then cover with plastic wrap and chill in the refrigerator for 2 hours, or until firm. Beat until just starting to hold soft peaks.

2 Preheat the oven to 350°F/180°C. Grease a deep 8-inch/20-cm round cake pan and line with parchment paper.

3 Put the butter and superfine sugar in a bowl and beat until light and fluffy. Gradually beat in the eggs. Sift the flour and cocoa into a bowl, then fold into the mixture, adding milk, if necessary, to make a dropping consistency.

4 Spoon into the prepared pan and bake in the preheated oven for 45–50 minutes, until a toothpick inserted into the center comes out clean. Let stand in the pan for 5 minutes, then transfer to a wire rack to cool completely.

5 To make the frosting, put the semisweet chocolate in a heatproof bowl set over a pan of gently simmering water until melted. Stir in the butter and cream. Let cool, stirring occasionally, until the mixture is a thick spreading consistency.

6 Slice the cake horizontally into three layers. Sandwich the layers together with the white chocolate filling. Cover the top and sides of the cake with the frosting and arrange the chocolate curls over the top. Sift the mixed confectioners' sugar and cocoa over the cake.

White Chocolate Coffee
Gâteau

Serves 8–10

ingredients

- 3 tbsp unsalted butter, plus extra for greasing
- 3 oz/85 g white chocolate
- ⅔ cup superfine sugar
- 4 extra large eggs, beaten
- 2 tbsp very strong black coffee
- 1 tsp vanilla extract
- heaping 1 cup all-purpose flour
- white chocolate curls, to decorate

frosting

- 6 oz/175 g white chocolate
- 6 tbsp unsalted butter
- generous ½ cup sour cream
- heaping 1 cup confectioners' sugar, sifted
- 1 tbsp coffee liqueur or very strong black coffee

1 Preheat the oven to 350°F/180°C. Grease two 8-inch/20-cm round cake pans and line with parchment paper.

2 Place the butter and chocolate in a bowl set over a saucepan of hot, but not simmering, water and let heat on very low heat until just melted. Stir to mix lightly, then remove from the heat.

3 Place the superfine sugar, eggs, coffee, and vanilla extract in a large bowl set over a saucepan of hot water and whisk hard with an electric mixer until the mixture is pale and thick enough to leave a trail when the beaters are lifted.

4 Remove from the heat, sift in the flour, and fold in lightly and evenly. Quickly fold in the butter-and-chocolate mixture, then divide the batter between the prepared pans.

5 Bake in the preheated oven for 25–30 minutes, until risen, golden brown, and springy to the touch. Cool in the pans for 2 minutes, then run a knife around the edges to loosen and turn out onto a wire rack to cool.

6 For the frosting, place the chocolate and butter in a bowl set over a saucepan of hot water and heat gently until melted. Remove from the heat, stir in the sour cream, then add the confectioners' sugar and coffee liqueur and mix until smooth. Chill the frosting for at least 30 minutes, stirring occasionally, until it becomes thick and glossy.

7 Use about one-third of the frosting to sandwich the cakes together. Spread the remainder over the top and sides, swirling with a spatula. Arrange the chocolate curls over the top of the cake and let set.

Chapter 2
Small Cakes & Bars

Vanilla Macaroons

Makes 16

ingredients
- ¾ cup ground almonds
- 1 cup confectioners' sugar
- 2 extra large egg whites
- ¼ cup superfine sugar
- ½ tsp vanilla extract

filling
- 4 tbsp unsalted butter, softened
- ½ tsp vanilla extract
- 1 cup confectioners' sugar, sifted

1 Place the ground almonds and confectioners' sugar in a food processor and process for 15 seconds. Sift the mixture into a bowl. Line two baking sheets with parchment paper.

2 Place the egg whites in a large bowl and whip until holding soft peaks. Gradually beat in the superfine sugar to make a firm, glossy meringue. Beat in the vanilla extract.

3 Using a spatula, fold the almond batter into the meringue one-third at a time. When all the dry ingredients are thoroughly incorporated, continue to cut and fold the mixture until it forms a shiny batter with a thick, ribbonlike consistency.

4 Pour the batter into a pastry bag fitted with a ½-inch/1-cm plain tip. Pipe 32 small circles onto the prepared baking sheets. Tap the baking sheets firmly onto a work surface to remove air bubbles. Let stand at room temperature for 30 minutes. Preheat the oven to 325°F/160°C.

5 Bake in the preheated oven for 10–15 minutes. Cool for 10 minutes. Carefully peel the macaroons off the parchment paper and let cool completely.

6 To make the filling, beat the butter and vanilla extract in a bowl until pale and fluffy. Gradually beat in the confectioners' sugar until smooth and creamy. Use to sandwich pairs of macaroons together.

Hazelnut Chocolate
Macaroons

Makes 16

ingredients
- ½ cup ground almonds
- ¼ cup finely ground hazelnuts, plus 1 tbsp chopped to decorate
- 1 cup confectioners' sugar
- 2 extra large egg whites
- ¼ cup superfine sugar
- generous ⅓ cup hazelnut and chocolate spread

1 Place the ground almonds, ground hazelnuts, and confectioners' sugar in a food processor and process for 15 seconds. Sift the mixture into a bowl. Line two baking sheets with parchment paper.

2 Place the egg whites in a large bowl and whip until holding soft peaks. Gradually beat in the superfine sugar until you have a firm, glossy meringue.

3 Using a spatula, fold the almond mixture into the meringue one-third at a time. When all the dry ingredients are thoroughly incorporated, continue to cut and fold the mixture until it forms a shiny batter with a thick, ribbonlike consistency.

4 Pour the batter into a pastry bag fitted with a ½-inch/1-cm plain tip. Pipe 32 small circles onto the prepared baking sheets. Tap the baking sheets firmly onto a work surface to remove air bubbles. Sprinkle over the chopped hazelnuts. Let stand at room temperature for 30 minutes. Preheat the oven to 325°F/160°C.

5 Bake in the preheated oven for 10–15 minutes. Cool for 10 minutes. Carefully peel the macaroons off the parchment paper and let cool completely.

6 Sandwich pairs of macaroons together with the hazelnut and chocolate spread.

Double Chocolate Muffins

Makes 12

ingredients

- scant ½ cup butter, softened
- scant ¾ cup superfine sugar
- ½ cup dark brown sugar
- 2 eggs
- ⅔ cup sour cream
- 5 tbsp milk
- 2 cups all-purpose flour
- 1 tsp baking soda
- 2 tbsp unsweetened cocoa
- 1 cup semisweet chocolate chips

1 Preheat the oven to 375°F/190°C. Place 12 baking cups in a muffin pan.

2 Put the butter, superfine sugar, and brown sugar into a bowl and beat well. Beat in the eggs, sour cream, and milk until thoroughly mixed. Sift the flour, baking soda, and cocoa into a separate bowl and stir into the mixture. Add the chocolate chips and mix well.

3 Spoon the batter into the baking cups. Bake in the preheated oven for 25–30 minutes. Remove from the oven and let cool for 10 minutes. Turn out onto a wire rack and let cool completely.

Warm Spiced Apple Pie
Cupcakes

Makes 12

ingredients
- 3½ tbsp butter, softened
- ⅓ cup raw brown sugar
- 1 egg, lightly beaten
- heaping 1 cup all-purpose flour
- 1½ tsp baking powder
- ½ tsp apple pie spice
- 1 large baking apple, peeled, cored, and finely chopped
- 1 tbsp orange juice

topping
- 5 tbsp all-purpose flour
- ½ tsp apple pie spice
- 2 tbsp butter
- ¼ cup superfine sugar

1 Preheat the oven to 350°F/180°C. Line a 12-hole muffin pan with 12 cupcake liners.

2 To make the topping, place the flour, apple pie spice, butter, and superfine sugar in a large bowl and rub in with your fingertips until the mixture resembles fine breadcrumbs. Set aside.

3 To make the cupcakes, place the butter and brown sugar in a large bowl and beat together until light and fluffy, then gradually beat in the egg. Sift in the flour, baking powder, and apple pie spice and fold into the mixture, then fold in the chopped apple and orange juice. Spoon the batter into the cupcake liners. Add the topping to cover the top of each cupcake and press down gently.

4 Bake in the preheated oven for 30 minutes, or until golden brown. Let the cupcakes cool in the pan for 2–3 minutes and serve warm, or let cool for 10 minutes and then transfer to a wire rack to cool completely.

Vanilla Frosted Cupcakes

Makes 12

ingredients

- ½ cup unsalted butter, softened
- heaping ½ cup superfine sugar
- 2 eggs, lightly beaten
- ¾ cup self-rising flour
- 1 tbsp milk
- candied rose petals, to decorate

frosting

- ¾ cup unsalted butter, softened
- 2 tsp vanilla extract
- 2 tbsp milk
- scant 2⅔ cups confectioners' sugar, sifted

1 Preheat the oven to 350°F/180°C. Put 12 cupcake liners in a 12-hole muffin pan.

2 Place the butter and superfine sugar in a bowl and beat together until light and fluffy. Gradually beat in the eggs. Sift in the flour and fold in gently using a metal spoon. Fold in the milk.

3 Spoon the batter into the cupcake liners. Bake in the preheated oven for 15–20 minutes, until golden brown and firm to the touch. Transfer to a wire rack and let cool.

4 To make the frosting, put the butter, vanilla extract, and milk in a large bowl. Using an electric mixer, beat the mixture until smooth. Gradually beat in the confectioners' sugar and continue beating for 2–3 minutes, until the frosting is light and creamy.

5 Spoon the frosting into a large pastry bag fitted with a large star tip and pipe swirls of the frosting onto the top of each cupcake. Decorate each cupcake with candied rose petals.

Chocolate Chip Brownies

Makes 12

ingredients

- 5½ oz/150 g semisweet chocolate, broken into pieces
- 1 cup butter, softened, plus extra for greasing
- heaping 1½ cups self-rising flour
- scant ⅔ cup superfine sugar
- 4 eggs, beaten
- ⅔ cup shelled pistachios, chopped
- 3½ oz/100 g white chocolate, coarsely chopped
- confectioners' sugar, for dusting

1 Preheat the oven to 350°F/180°C. Grease a 9-inch/23-cm square baking pan and line with parchment paper.

2 Place the chocolate and butter in a heatproof bowl set over a pan of simmering water. Stir until melted, then let cool slightly.

3 Sift the flour into a separate bowl and stir in the superfine sugar.

4 Stir the beaten eggs into the chocolate mixture, then pour the mixture into the flour and sugar and beat well. Stir in the pistachios and white chocolate, then pour the batter into the prepared pan, using a spatula to spread it evenly.

5 Bake in the preheated oven for 30–35 minutes, or until firm to the touch around the edges. Let cool in the pan for 20 minutes. Turn out onto a wire rack. Dust with confectioners' sugar and let cool completely. Cut into 12 pieces and serve.

Rocky Road Brownies

Makes 16

ingredients

- scant 1 cup all-purpose flour, plus extra for dusting
- scant ¾ cup superfine sugar
- 3 tbsp unsweetened cocoa
- ½ tsp baking powder
- 1 cup butter, melted, plus extra for greasing
- 2 eggs, beaten
- 1 tsp vanilla extract
- ⅓ cup candied cherries, cut into fourths
- ¾ cup blanched almonds, chopped
- heaping 1 cup chopped marshmallows, to decorate

frosting

- 1¾ cups confectioners' sugar
- 2 tbsp unsweetened cocoa
- 3 tbsp evaporated milk
- ½ tsp vanilla extract

1 Preheat the oven to 325°F/160°C. Grease a shallow 9-inch/23-cm square cake pan and sprinkle lightly with flour.

2 Sift together the flour, superfine sugar, cocoa, and baking powder and make a well in the center. Stir in the melted butter, eggs, and vanilla extract and beat well to mix thoroughly.

3 Stir in the cherries and almonds. Pour into the prepared pan and bake in the preheated oven for 35–40 minutes, until just firm on top. Let cool in the pan.

4 Meanwhile, make the frosting. Place all the ingredients in a large bowl and beat well to mix to a smooth, just spreading consistency.

5 Spread the cooled brownies with the frosting, swirling lightly, and sprinkle with marshmallows. Let stand until the frosting sets, then cut into squares.

Coconut Squares

Makes 16

ingredients

- 6 eggs
- ¾ cup superfine sugar
- 1½ cups all-purpose flour
- ¼ cup unsalted butter, melted, plus extra for greasing
- 3 cups dry unsweetened coconut

frosting

- 4½ cups confectioners' sugar
- ⅓ cup unsweetened cocoa
- ⅓ cup boiling water
- 5 tbsp unsalted butter, melted

1 Preheat the oven to 350°F/180°C. Grease an 8-inch/20-cm square cake pan and line with parchment paper.

2 Place the eggs and superfine sugar in a large bowl set over a saucepan of gently simmering water. Whisk until pale and thick enough to leave a trail when the whisk is lifted.

3 Remove from the heat, sift in the flour, and fold in evenly. Fold in the melted butter. Pour into the prepared pan and bake in the preheated oven for 35–40 minutes, or until risen, golden, and springy to the touch.

4 Let cool in the pan for 2–3 minutes, then turn out onto a wire rack to finish cooling. When cold, cut the cake into 16 squares.

5 For the frosting, sift together the confectioners' sugar and cocoa into a bowl and stir in the water and butter, mixing until smooth. Spread out the dry unsweetened coconut on a large plate. Dip each piece of cake into the frosting, using two spatulas to turn and coat evenly. Place in the dry unsweetened coconut and turn to coat evenly. Place on a sheet of parchment paper and let set.

Malted Chocolate Bars

Makes 16

ingredients
- 6 tbsp butter,
  plus extra for greasing
- 2 tbsp light corn syrup
- 2 tbsp malted chocolate powder
- 2 cups malted milk
  cookie crumbs
- 2¾ oz/75 g semisweet chocolate,
  broken into pieces
- 2 tbsp confectioners' sugar
- 2 tbsp milk

1 Grease a shallow 7-inch/18-cm round cake pan and line with parchment paper.

2 Place the butter, corn syrup, and malted chocolate powder in a small pan and heat gently, stirring all the time until the butter has melted and the mixture is well combined.

3 Stir the cookie crumbs into the butter mixture and mix well. (You can make the crumbs by crushing the cookies in a plastic bag with a rolling pin.)

4 Press the mixture into the prepared pan and then chill in the refrigerator until firm.

5 Place the chocolate pieces in a small heatproof bowl with the sugar and milk. Place the bowl over a pan of gently simmering water and stir until the chocolate melts and the mixture is combined.

6 Spread the chocolate topping over the cookie base and let the topping set in the pan. Using a sharp knife, cut into triangles to serve.

Macadamia Nut Caramel Squares

Makes 16

ingredients
- 1 cup macadamia nuts
- 2 cups all-purpose flour
- 1 cup brown sugar
- ½ cup butter

topping
- ½ cup butter
- ½ cup brown sugar
- 1½ cups milk chocolate chips

1 Preheat the oven to 350°F/180°C. Halve the macadamia nuts. To make the bottom of the squares, beat together the flour, sugar, and butter until the mixture resembles fine breadcrumbs.

2 Press the mixture into the bottom of a 12 x 8-inch/30 x 20-cm jelly roll pan. Sprinkle over the nuts.

3 To make the topping, put the butter and sugar in a pan and, stirring continuously, slowly bring the mixture to a boil. Boil for 1 minute, stirring continuously, then carefully pour the mixture over the macadamia nuts.

4 Bake in the preheated oven for about 20 minutes, until the caramel topping is bubbling. Remove from the oven and immediately sprinkle the chocolate chips evenly on top. Let stand for 2–3 minutes, until the chocolate chips start to melt, then, using the blade of a knife, swirl the chocolate over the top. Let cool in the pan, then cut into bars or squares.

Chocolate Caramel
Shortbread

Makes 12

ingredients
- ½ cup butter, plus extra for greasing
- heaping 1 cup all-purpose flour
- heaping ¼ cup superfine sugar

filling & topping
- ¾ cup butter
- heaping ½ cup superfine sugar
- 3 tbsp light corn syrup
- 14 oz/400 g canned sweetened condensed milk
- 7 oz/200 g semisweet chocolate, broken into pieces

1 Preheat the oven to 350°F/180°C. Grease a shallow 9-inch/23-cm square cake pan and line with parchment paper.

2 Place the butter, flour, and sugar in a food processor and process until it starts to bind together. Press into the prepared pan and level the top. Bake in the preheated oven for 20–25 minutes, or until golden.

3 Meanwhile, make the caramel filling. Place the butter, sugar, corn syrup, and condensed milk in a heavy-bottom saucepan. Heat gently until the sugar has dissolved. Bring to a boil, then reduce the heat and let simmer for 6–8 minutes, stirring, until very thick. Pour over the shortbread and let chill in the refrigerator for 2 hours, or until firm.

4 Place the chocolate in a heatproof bowl set over a saucepan of gently simmering water and stir until melted. Let cool slightly, then spread over the caramel. Let chill in the refrigerator for 2 hours, or until set. Cut the shortbread into 12 pieces using a sharp knife and serve.

Almond Biscotti

Makes about 35

ingredients
- 1¾ cups whole blanched almonds
- 1⅔ cups all-purpose flour, plus extra for dusting
- heaping ¾ cup superfine sugar, plus extra for sprinkling
- 1 tsp baking powder
- ½ tsp ground cinnamon
- 2 eggs
- 2 tsp vanilla extract

1 Preheat the oven to 350°F/180°C. Line two baking sheets with parchment paper.

2 Very coarsely chop the almonds, leaving some whole. Mix the flour, sugar, baking powder, and cinnamon together in a mixing bowl. Stir in the almonds.

3 Beat the eggs with the vanilla extract in a small bowl, then add to the flour mixture and mix together to form a firm dough. Turn the dough out onto a lightly floured surface and knead lightly.

4 Divide the dough in half and shape each piece into a log, roughly 2 inches/5 cm wide. Transfer to the prepared baking sheets and sprinkle with sugar. Bake in the preheated oven for 20–25 minutes, until firm.

5 Remove from the oven and let cool slightly, then transfer to a cutting board and cut into ½-inch/1-cm slices. Meanwhile, reduce the oven temperature to 325°F/160°C.

6 Arrange the slices, cut-sides down, on the baking sheets. Bake in the oven for 15–20 minutes, until dry and crispy. Transfer to a wire rack to cool. Store in an airtight container to keep crisp.

Nutty Granola Bars

Makes 16

ingredients
- scant 2¾ cups rolled oats
- ¾ cup chopped hazelnuts
- heaping ⅓ cup all-purpose flour
- ½ cup butter,
  plus extra for greasing
- 2 tbsp light corn syrup
- scant ½ cup brown sugar

1 Preheat the oven to 350°F/180°C, then grease a 9-inch/23-cm square cake pan. Place the rolled oats, chopped hazelnuts, and flour in a large mixing bowl and stir together.

2 Place the butter, corn syrup, and sugar in a pan over low heat and stir until melted. Pour onto the dry ingredients and mix well. Turn into the prepared pan and smooth the surface with the back of a spoon.

3 Bake in the preheated oven for 20–25 minutes, or until golden and firm to the touch. Mark into 16 pieces and let cool in the pan. When completely cooled, cut through with a sharp knife and serve.

Chocolate Peanut Butter Squares

Makes 20

ingredients

- 10½ oz/300 g milk chocolate
- 2½ cups all-purpose flour
- 1 tsp baking powder
- 1 cup butter
- 1¾ cups light brown sugar
- 2 cups rolled oats
- ½ cup chopped mixed nuts
- 1 egg, beaten
- 14 oz/400 g canned sweetened condensed milk
- ⅓ cup chunky peanut butter

1 Preheat the oven to 350°F/180°C. Finely chop the chocolate. Sift the flour and baking powder into a large bowl. Add the butter to the flour mixture and rub in using your fingertips until the mixture resembles breadcrumbs. Stir in the sugar, rolled oats, and chopped nuts.

2 Put a quarter of the mixture into a bowl and stir in the chocolate. Set aside.

3 Stir the egg into the remaining mixture, then press into the bottom of a 12 x 8-inch/30 x 20-cm cake pan. Bake in the preheated oven for 15 minutes.

4 Meanwhile, mix the condensed milk and peanut butter together. Pour into the cake pan and spread evenly, then sprinkle the reserved chocolate mixture on top and press down lightly.

5 Return to the oven and bake for an additional 20 minutes, until golden brown. Let cool in the pan, then cut into squares.

White Chocolate & Apricot Squares

Makes 12

ingredients

- heaping ½ cup butter, plus extra for greasing
- 6 oz/175 g white chocolate, chopped
- 4 eggs
- ½ cup superfine sugar
- 1¾ cups all-purpose flour, sifted
- 1 tsp baking powder
- pinch of salt
- ½ cup chopped plumped dried apricots

1 Preheat the oven to 350°F/180°C. Grease an 8-inch/20-cm square cake pan and line with parchment paper.

2 Melt the butter and chocolate in a heatproof bowl set over a pan of gently simmering water. Stir frequently with a wooden spoon until the mixture is smooth and glossy. Let the mixture cool slightly.

3 Beat the eggs and superfine sugar into the butter-and-chocolate mixture until well combined.

4 Fold in the flour, baking powder, salt, and chopped dried apricots and mix thoroughly.

5 Spoon the batter into the prepared pan and bake in the preheated oven for about 25–30 minutes. The center of the cake may not be completely firm, but it will set as it cools. Let stand in the pan to cool.

6 When the cake is completely cool, turn it out carefully and slice into bars or small squares.

Viennese Shortcakes

Makes 12

ingredients

- 1 cup unsalted butter, softened
- 1 tsp vanilla extract
- ¾ cup confectioners' sugar, plus extra for dusting
- 1¼ cups self-rising flour
- heaping ⅓ cup cornstarch
- 2 tbsp strawberry jelly

1 Preheat the oven to 350°F/180°C. Put 12 baking cups in a 12-hole muffin pan.

2 Place the butter and vanilla extract in a large bowl and, using an electric mixer, beat together until the butter is very soft. Sift in the confectioners' sugar and beat thoroughly.

3 Sift together the flour and cornstarch and stir into the mixture until smooth. Spoon the batter into a large pastry bag fitted with a large star tip and pipe swirls of the batter into the baking cups, leaving a slight dip in the center of each one.

4 Bake in the preheated oven for 15–20 minutes, until golden. Let the shortcakes cool in the pan for 15 minutes, then transfer to a wire rack and let cool completely.

5 Spoon a little jelly into the center of each shortcake and dust with confectioners' sugar.

Chocolate Whoopie Pies

Makes 10

ingredients

- 1¼ cups all-purpose flour
- 1½ tsp baking soda
- scant ½ cup unsweetened cocoa
- large pinch of salt
- 6 tbsp butter, softened
- heaping ⅓ cup vegetable shortening
- ¾ cup dark brown sugar
- 1 extra large egg, beaten
- 1 tsp vanilla extract
- ⅔ cup milk

marshmallow filling

- 8 oz/225 g white marshmallows
- 4 tbsp milk
- ½ cup vegetable shortening
- ½ cup confectioners' sugar, sifted

1 Preheat the oven to 350°F/180°C. Line two or three large cookie sheets with parchment paper. Sift together the flour, baking soda, cocoa, and salt.

2 Place the butter, vegetable shortening, and brown sugar in a large bowl and beat with an electric mixer until pale and fluffy. Beat in the egg and vanilla extract followed by half of the flour mixture and then the milk. Stir in the rest of the flour mixture and mix until thoroughly incorporated.

3 Pipe or spoon 20 mounds of the batter onto the prepared cookie sheets, spaced well apart to allow for spreading. Bake in the preheated oven, one sheet at a time, for 12–14 minutes until risen and just firm to the touch. Cool for 5 minutes, then, using a palette knife, transfer to a wire rack to cool completely.

4 For the filling, place the marshmallows and milk in a heatproof bowl set over a pan of simmering water. Heat until the marshmallows have melted, stirring occasionally. Remove from the heat and let cool.

5 Place the vegetable shortening and confectioners' sugar in a bowl and beat together until smooth and creamy. Add the creamed mixture to the marshmallow and beat for 1–2 minutes, until fluffy.

6 To assemble, spread the filling over the flat side of half the cakes. Top with the remaining cakes.

Hazelnut Bars

Makes 16

ingredients
- 1¼ cups all-purpose flour
- pinch of salt
- 1 tsp baking powder
- 5 tbsp butter, diced, plus extra for greasing
- 1 cup brown sugar
- 1 egg, beaten
- 4 tbsp milk
- 1 cup hazelnuts, halved
- brown sugar cubes, crushed, for sprinkling (optional)

1 Preheat the oven to 350°F/180°C. Grease a 9-inch/23-cm square cake pan and line with parchment paper.

2 Sift the flour, salt, and baking powder into a large mixing bowl. Rub in the butter with your fingers until the mixture resembles fine breadcrumbs. Stir in the brown sugar.

3 Add the egg, milk, and nuts to the mixture and stir well, until thoroughly combined.

4 Spoon the batter into the prepared cake pan and level the surface. Sprinkle with crushed sugar cubes, if using.

5 Bake in the preheated oven for about 25 minutes, or until the mixture is firm to the touch when pressed with a finger.

6 Let cool for 10 minutes, then loosen the edges with a round-bladed knife and turn out onto a wire rack. Cut into bars or squares.

Date, Pistachio & Honey
Slices

Makes 12

ingredients

- 1½ cups chopped, pitted dried dates
- 2 tbsp lemon juice
- 2 tbsp water
- ¾ cup pistachio nuts, chopped
- 2 tbsp honey
- milk, to glaze

pastry

- 2 cups all-purpose flour, plus extra for dusting
- 2 tbsp superfine sugar
- ⅔ cup butter
- 4–5 tbsp cold water, to mix

1 Preheat the oven to 400°F/200°C. Put the dates, lemon juice, and water in a pan and bring to a boil, stirring. Remove from the heat. Stir in the pistachios and 1 tablespoon of honey and let cool.

2 For the pastry dough, put the flour, sugar, and butter in a food processor and process to fine breadcrumbs.

3 Mix in just enough cold water to bind to a soft, nonsticky dough. Roll out the dough on a floured surface to two 12 x 8 inch/30 x 20 cm rectangles. Place one rectangle on a baking sheet.

4 Spread the date-and-nut mixture to within ½ inch/1 cm of the edge. Top with the remaining dough. Press to seal, trim the edges, and mark into 12 slices. Glaze with milk.

5 Bake in the preheated oven for 20–25 minutes, brush with the remaining honey, and cool on a wire rack. Cut into 12 slices and serve.

Chapter 3
Cookies

Chocolate Chip Cookies

Makes 18

ingredients

- ½ cup soft margarine, plus extra for greasing
- 1½ cups all-purpose flour, sifted
- 1 tsp baking powder
- scant ⅔ cup light brown sugar
- ¼ cup superfine sugar
- ½ tsp vanilla extract
- 1 egg
- ⅔ cup semisweet chocolate chips

1 Preheat the oven to 375°F/190°C. Grease two cookie sheets.

2 Place all the ingredients in a large mixing bowl and beat until they are thoroughly combined.

3 Place tablespoonfuls of the mixture onto the cookie sheets, spacing them well apart to leave room for spreading during cooking.

4 Bake in the preheated oven for 10–12 minutes, until the cookies are golden brown.

5 Using a spatula, transfer the cookies to a wire rack to cool completely before serving.

Classic Oatmeal Cookies

Makes 30

ingredients

- ¾ cup butter or margarine, plus extra for greasing
- scant 1⅓ cups raw brown sugar
- 1 egg
- 4 tbsp water
- 1 tsp vanilla extract
- 4⅓ cups rolled oats
- 1 cup all-purpose flour
- 1 tsp salt
- ½ tsp baking soda

1 Preheat the oven to 350°F/180°C. Grease a large cookie sheet.

2 Cream the butter and sugar together in a large mixing bowl. Beat in the egg, water, and vanilla extract until the mixture is smooth.

3 In a separate bowl, mix the oats, flour, salt, and baking soda together. Gradually stir the oat mixture into the butter mixture until thoroughly combined.

4 Put tablespoonfuls of the mixture onto the prepared cookie sheet, spaced well apart. Transfer to the preheated oven and bake for 15 minutes, or until the cookies are golden brown.

5 Remove the cookies from the oven and place on a wire rack to cool before serving.

Peanut Butter Cookies

Makes 26

ingredients
- ½ cup butter, softened, plus extra for greasing
- scant ½ cup chunky peanut butter
- heaping ½ cup superfine sugar
- heaping ½ cup light brown sugar
- 1 egg, beaten
- ½ tsp vanilla extract
- ⅔ cup all-purpose flour
- ½ tsp baking soda
- ½ tsp baking powder
- pinch of salt
- 1½ cups rolled oats

1 Preheat the oven to 350°F/180°C. Grease three cookie sheets.

2 Place the butter and peanut butter in a bowl and beat together. Beat in the superfine sugar and brown sugar, then gradually beat in the egg and vanilla extract.

3 Sift the flour, baking soda, baking powder, and salt into the bowl and stir in the oats.

4 Place spoonfuls of the cookie dough onto the cookie sheets, spaced well apart. Flatten slightly with a fork.

5 Bake in the preheated oven for 12 minutes, or until lightly browned. Let cool on the cookie sheets for 2 minutes, then transfer to wire racks to cool completely.

Almond Cookies with a
Cherry on Top

Makes 25

ingredients

- heaping ¾ cup butter, diced, plus extra for greasing
- ½ cup superfine sugar
- ½ tsp almond extract
- 2 cups self-rising flour
- heaping ¼ cup ground almonds
- 25 candied cherries (total weight about 4½ oz/125 g)

1 Preheat the oven to 350°F/180°C. Grease several large cookie sheets.

2 Place the butter in a large saucepan and heat gently until melted. Remove from the heat. Add the sugar and almond extract to the pan and stir together. Add the flour and ground almonds and mix to form a smooth dough.

3 Roll small pieces of the dough between your hands into smooth balls to make 25 in total. Place on the cookie sheets, spaced well apart, and flatten slightly with your hands, then press a cherry gently into the center of each cookie. Bake in the preheated oven for 10–15 minutes, or until golden brown.

4 Let cool for 2–3 minutes on the cookie sheets, then transfer the cookies to a wire rack to cool completely.

Chocolate Chip & Cinnamon Cookies

Makes about 30

ingredients
- 1 cup butter, softened
- scant ¾ cup superfine sugar
- 1 egg yolk, lightly beaten
- 2 tsp orange extract
- 2½ cups all-purpose flour
- pinch of salt
- heaping ½ cup semisweet chocolate chips

cinnamon coating
- 1½ tbsp superfine sugar
- 1½ tbsp ground cinnamon

1 Preheat the oven to 375°F/190°C. Line two cookie sheets with parchment paper.

2 Put the butter and sugar into a bowl and mix well with a wooden spoon, then beat in the egg yolk and orange extract. Sift together the flour and salt into the mixture, add the chocolate chips, and stir until thoroughly combined.

3 For the coating, mix together the sugar and cinnamon in a shallow dish. Scoop out tablespoons of the cookie dough, roll them into balls, then roll them in the cinnamon mixture to coat. Put them on the prepared cookie sheets, spaced well apart.

4 Bake in the preheated oven for 12–15 minutes. Let cool on the cookie sheets for 5–10 minutes, then, using a metal spatula, carefully transfer to wire racks to cool completely.

Orange Cookies

Makes about 30

ingredients
- ⅓ cup butter, softened
- ⅓ cup superfine sugar
- 1 egg
- 1 tbsp milk
- 2 cups all-purpose flour
- ¼ cup unsweetened cocoa

icing
- 1 cup confectioners' sugar, sifted
- 3 tbsp orange juice
- a little semisweet chocolate, melted

1 Preheat the oven to 350°F/180°C. Line two cookie sheets with parchment paper.

2 Beat together the butter and sugar until light and fluffy. Beat in the egg and milk until well combined. Sift together the flour and unsweetened cocoa and gradually mix together to form a soft dough. Use your fingers to incorporate the last of the flour and to bring the dough together.

3 Roll out the dough onto a lightly floured surface until ¼ inch/5 mm thick. Using a 2-inch/5-cm fluted round cutter, cut out as many cookies as you can. Reroll the dough trimmings and cut out more cookies.

4 Place the cookies on the prepared cookie sheets and bake in the preheated oven for 10–12 minutes, or until golden.

5 Let the cookies cool on the cookie sheets for a few minutes, then transfer to a wire rack to cool completely.

6 To make the icing, place the confectioners' sugar in a bowl and stir in enough orange juice to form a thin icing that will coat the back of a spoon. Spread the icing over the cookies and let set. Drizzle with melted chocolate. Let the chocolate set before serving.

Chocolate Spread & Hazelnut Drops

Makes about 30

ingredients

- 1 cup butter, softened
- scant ¾ cup superfine sugar
- 1 egg yolk, lightly beaten
- 2 tsp vanilla extract
- 2 cups all-purpose flour
- ½ cup unsweetened cocoa
- pinch of salt
- ½ cup ground hazelnuts
- ⅓ cup semisweet chocolate chips
- 4 tbsp chocolate and hazelnut spread

1 Preheat the oven to 375°F/190°C. Line two cookie sheets with parchment paper.

2 Put the butter and sugar into a bowl and mix well with a wooden spoon, then beat in the egg yolk and vanilla extract. Sift together the flour, unsweetened cocoa, and salt into the mixture, add the ground hazelnuts and chocolate chips, and stir until thoroughly combined.

3 Scoop out tablespoons of the mixture and shape into balls with your hands, then put them on the prepared cookie sheets, spaced well apart. Use the dampened handle of a wooden spoon to make a hollow in the center of each cookie.

4 Bake in the preheated oven for 12–15 minutes. Let cool on the cookie sheets for 5–10 minutes, then, using a metal spatula, carefully transfer the cookies to wire racks to cool completely. When they have cooled down completely, fill the hollows in the center with chocolate and hazelnut spread.

Pecan & Maple Cookies

Makes 18

ingredients

- ½ cup pecans
- ½ cup butter, softened, plus extra for greasing
- 2 tbsp maple syrup
- scant ½ cup light brown sugar
- 1 extra large egg yolk, lightly beaten
- heaping ¾ cup self-rising flour

1 Preheat the oven to 375°F/190°C. Grease two cookies sheets. Reserve 18 pecan halves and coarsely chop the rest.

2 Place the butter, maple syrup, and sugar in a bowl and beat together with a wooden spoon until light and fluffy. Beat in the egg yolk. Sift over the flour and add the chopped pecans. Mix to a stiff dough.

3 Place 18 golf ball-size spoonfuls of the mixture onto the prepared cookie sheets, spaced well apart. Top each with a reserved pecan, pressing down gently.

4 Bake in the preheated oven for 10–12 minutes, until light golden brown. Let cool on the cookie sheets for 10 minutes, then transfer to a wire rack to cool completely.

Banana & Raisin
Cookies

Makes about 30

ingredients

- 2 tbsp raisins
- ½ cup orange juice or rum
- 1 cup butter, softened
- ¾ cup superfine sugar
- 1 egg yolk, lightly beaten
- 2 cups all-purpose flour
- pinch of salt
- ¾ cup dried bananas, finely chopped

1 Place the raisins in a bowl, pour in the orange juice or rum, and let soak for 30 minutes. Drain the raisins, reserving any remaining liquid.

2 Preheat the oven to 375°F/190°C. Line two large cookie sheets with parchment paper. Place the butter and sugar in a large bowl and beat together until light and fluffy, then beat in the egg yolk and 2 teaspoons of the reserved orange juice. Sift together the flour and salt into the mixture, add the raisins and dried bananas, and stir until combined.

3 Place tablespoons of the mixture in mounds on the cookie sheets, spaced well apart, then flatten them gently.

4 Bake in the preheated oven for 12–15 minutes, or until golden. Let cool on the cookie sheets for 5–10 minutes, then transfer the cookies to wire racks to cool completely.

Coconut & Cranberry
Cookies

Makes about 30

ingredients

- 1 cup butter, softened
- scant ¾ cup superfine sugar
- 1 egg yolk, lightly beaten
- 2 tsp vanilla extract
- 2½ cups all-purpose flour
- pinch of salt
- ½ cup unsweetened dried shredded coconut
- ½ cup dried cranberries

1 Preheat the oven to 375°F/190°C. Line two cookie sheets with parchment paper.

2 Put the butter and sugar into a bowl and mix well with a wooden spoon, then beat in the egg yolk and vanilla extract.

3 Sift together the flour and salt into the mixture, add the coconut and cranberries, and stir until thoroughly combined. Scoop up tablespoons of the dough and place in mounds on the prepared cookie sheets, spaced well apart.

4 Bake in the preheated oven for 12–15 minutes, until golden brown. Let cool on the cookie sheets for 5–10 minutes, then, using a metal spatula, carefully transfer to wire racks to cool completely.

Chunky Apricot & Pecan Cookies

Makes 16

- ⅓ cup sunflower spread, plus extra for greasing
- ⅓ cup light brown sugar
- 1 egg, beaten
- ½ tsp grated nutmeg
- 1 tsp vanilla extract
- 1⅔ cups self-rising flour
- 1⅓ cups coarsely chopped plumped dried apricots
- ¾ cup coarsely chopped pecans

1 Preheat the oven to 400°F/200°C. Grease two cookie sheets.

2 Place the spread, sugar, egg, nutmeg, and vanilla in a bowl and beat until smooth. Stir in the flour, apricots, and pecans, mixing to form a soft dough.

3 Use a tablespoon to place mounds of dough on the cookie sheets, pressing them with a fork to flatten slightly.

4 Bake in the preheated oven for 12–15 minutes, or until golden brown. Transfer to a wire rack to cool.

Gingersnaps

Makes 30

ingredients

- 2½ cups self-rising flour
- pinch of salt
- 1 cup superfine sugar
- 1 tbsp ground ginger
- 1 tsp baking soda
- ½ cup butter, plus extra for greasing
- ¼ cup light corn syrup
- 1 egg, lightly beaten
- 1 tsp grated orange rind

1 Preheat the oven to 325°F/160°C. Grease several cookie sheets.

2 Sift together the flour, salt, sugar, ground ginger, and baking soda into a large mixing bowl.

3 Heat the butter and corn syrup together in a saucepan over very low heat until the butter has melted.

4 Let the butter mixture cool slightly, then pour it onto the dry ingredients. Add the egg and orange rind and mix together thoroughly.

5 Using your hands, carefully shape the dough into 30 even-size balls. Place the balls on the prepared cookie sheets, spaced well apart, then flatten them slightly with your fingers.

6 Bake in the preheated oven for 15–20 minutes. Carefully transfer the cookies to a wire rack to cool and crisp.

Florentine Cookies

Makes 18

ingredients

- ½ cup butter, softened, plus extra for greasing
- heaping ½ cup superfine sugar
- 1 egg, beaten
- 1¼ cups all-purpose flour
- ½ tsp baking soda
- ¼ cup slivered almonds, lightly crushed
- ¼ cup candied cherries, chopped
- 1 cup mixed peel
- ⅓ cup raisins
- 3 oz/85 g semisweet chocolate, melted

1 Preheat the oven to 375°F/190°C. Grease two cookie sheets.

2 Place the butter and sugar in a bowl and beat together until pale and fluffy. Beat in the egg. Sift in the flour and baking soda and mix to a soft dough.

3 Mix together the almonds, cherries, mixed peel, and raisins. Stir half into the cookie dough. Place 18 heaping spoonfuls of the dough onto the cookie sheets, spaced well apart. Sprinkle with the rest of the fruit-and-nut mixture.

4 Bake in the preheated oven for 10–12 minutes, until pale golden. Let cool on sheets for 10 minutes, then transfer to a wire rack to cool completely.

5 Use a teaspoon to drizzle melted chocolate over each cookie. Let set.

Spiced Rum Cookies

Makes 18

ingredients

- ¾ cup unsalted butter, plus extra for greasing
- 1 cup dark brown sugar
- 2 cups all-purpose flour
- pinch of salt
- ½ tsp baking soda
- 1 tsp ground cinnamon
- ½ tsp ground coriander
- ½ tsp ground nutmeg
- ¼ tsp ground cloves
- 2 tbsp dark rum

1 Preheat the oven to 350°F/180°C. Grease two cookie sheets.

2 Cream together the butter and sugar and beat until light and fluffy.

3 Sift the flour, salt, baking soda, cinnamon, coriander, nutmeg, and cloves into the creamed mixture.

4 Pour the dark rum into the creamed mixture and stir well.

5 Using 2 teaspoons, place small mounds of the mixture onto the cookie sheets, spaced well apart. Flatten each one slightly with the back of a spoon.

6 Bake in the preheated oven for 10–12 minutes, or until golden. Let the cookies cool and become crisp on wire racks before serving.

Oat, Raisin & Hazelnut
Cookies

Makes about 30

ingredients

- scant ½ cup raisins, chopped
- ½ cup orange juice
- 1 cup butter, softened
- scant ¾ cup superfine sugar
- 1 egg yolk, lightly beaten
- 2 tsp vanilla extract
- 2 cups all-purpose flour
- pinch of salt
- ½ cup rolled oats
- ½ cup chopped hazelnuts, plus whole hazelnuts to decorate

1 Preheat the oven to 375°F/190°C. Line two cookie sheets with parchment paper. Put the raisins in a bowl, add the orange juice, and let soak for 10 minutes.

2 Put the butter and sugar into a bowl and mix well with a wooden spoon, then beat in the egg yolk and vanilla extract. Sift together the flour and salt into the mixture and add the oats and chopped hazelnuts. Drain the raisins, add them to the mixture, and stir until thoroughly combined.

3 Scoop up tablespoons of the mixture and put them in mounds on the prepared cookie sheets, spaced well apart. Flatten slightly and place a whole hazelnut in the center of each cookie.

4 Bake in the preheated oven for 12–15 minutes, until golden brown. Let cool on the cookie sheets for 5–10 minutes, then, using a metal spatula, carefully transfer the cookies to wire racks to cool completely.

Crunchy Granola Cookies

Makes 24

ingredients

- ½ cup unsalted butter, softened, plus extra for greasing
- ½ cup raw brown sugar
- 1 tbsp honey
- heaping ¾ cup self-rising flour
- pinch of salt
- ⅓ cup plumped dried apricots, chopped
- heaping ⅓ cup dried figs, chopped
- 1⅓ cups rolled oats
- 1 tsp milk (optional)
- ¼ cup raisins or cranberries
- scant ½ cup walnut halves, chopped

1 Preheat the oven to 325°F/160°C. Grease two large cookie sheets. Place the butter, sugar, and honey in a saucepan and heat over low heat until melted. Mix to combine.

2 Sift together the flour and salt into a large bowl and stir in the apricots, figs, and oats. Pour in the butter-and-sugar mixture and mix to form a dough. If it is too stiff, add a little milk.

3 Divide the dough into 24 pieces and roll each piece into a ball. Place 12 balls on each cookie sheet and press flat to a diameter of 2½ inches/6 cm. Mix the raisins and walnuts together and press into the cookies.

4 Bake in the preheated oven for 15 minutes, swapping the sheets halfway through. Let cool on the cookie sheets.

Lemon Chocolate
Pinwheels

Makes 40

ingredients

- ¾ cup butter, softened, plus extra for greasing
- 1⅓ cups superfine sugar
- 1 egg, beaten
- 3 cups all-purpose flour, plus extra for dusting
- 1 oz/25 g semisweet chocolate, broken into pieces
- grated rind of 1 lemon

1 Grease and flour several cookie sheets. In a large mixing bowl, cream together the butter and sugar until light and fluffy.

2 Gradually add the beaten egg to the creamed mixture, beating well after each addition. Sift the flour into the creamed mixture and mix thoroughly until a soft dough forms.

3 Transfer half of the dough to another bowl. Put the chocolate in a heatproof bowl set over a pan of gently simmering water until melted. Cool slightly. Beat the chocolate into one half of the dough.

4 Stir the grated lemon rind into the other half of the plain dough. On a lightly floured surface, roll out the doughs to form two rectangles. Lay the lemon dough on top of the chocolate dough. Roll up tightly, using a sheet of parchment paper to guide you. Chill the dough for 1 hour.

5 Preheat the oven to 375°F/190°C. Cut the roll into 40 slices, place them on the cookie sheets, and bake in the preheated oven for 10–12 minutes, or until lightly golden. Transfer the pinwheels to a wire rack and let cool completely before serving.

Chocolate & Orange
Sandwich Cookies

Makes about 15

ingredients
- 1 cup butter, softened
- scant ¾ cup superfine sugar
- 2 tsp finely grated orange rind
- 1 egg yolk, lightly beaten
- 2 tsp vanilla extract
- 2¼ cups all-purpose flour
- ¼ cup unsweetened cocoa
- pinch of salt
- 3½ oz/100 g semisweet chocolate, finely chopped

chocolate filling
- ½ cup heavy cream
- 7 oz/200 g white chocolate, broken into pieces
- 1 tsp orange extract

1 Preheat the oven to 375°F/190°C. Line two cookie sheets with parchment paper.

2 Put the butter, sugar, and orange rind into a bowl and mix well with a wooden spoon, then beat in the egg yolk and vanilla extract. Sift together the flour, cocoa, and salt into the mixture, add the chopped chocolate, and stir until thoroughly combined.

3 Scoop up tablespoons of the dough, roll into balls, and put on the prepared cookie sheets, spaced well apart. Gently flatten and smooth the tops with the back of a spoon.

4 Bake in the preheated oven for 10–15 minutes, until light golden brown. Let cool on the cookie sheets for 5–10 minutes, then, using a metal spatula, carefully transfer to wire racks to cool completely.

5 To make the filling, bring the cream to a boil in a small saucepan, then remove the saucepan from the heat. Stir in the white chocolate until the mixture is smooth, then stir in the orange extract. When the mixture is completely cool, use to sandwich the cookies together in pairs.

Crunchy Nut & Honey
Sandwich Cookies

Makes about 30

ingredients
- 1 cup butter, softened
- scant ¾ cup superfine sugar
- 1 egg yolk, lightly beaten
- 2 tsp vanilla extract
- 2½ cups all-purpose flour
- pinch of salt
- ⅓ cup macadamia nuts, cashew nuts, or pine nuts, chopped

filling
- ⅓ cup butter, softened
- ¾ cup confectioners' sugar
- ⅓ cup clover or other set honey

1 Preheat the oven to 375°F/190°C. Line two cookie sheets with parchment paper.

2 Put the butter and superfine sugar into a bowl and mix well with a wooden spoon, then beat in the egg yolk and vanilla extract. Sift together the flour and salt into the mixture and stir until thoroughly combined.

3 Scoop up tablespoons of the dough and roll into balls. Put half of them on a prepared cookie sheet, spaced well apart, and flatten gently. Spread out the nuts in a shallow dish and dip one side of the remaining dough balls into them, then place on the other cookie sheet, nut side uppermost, and flatten gently.

4 Bake in the preheated oven for 10–15 minutes, until light golden brown. Let cool on the cookie sheets for 5–10 minutes, then, using a metal spatula, carefully transfer to wire racks to cool completely.

5 For the filling, beat the butter with the confectioners' sugar and honey until creamy and thoroughly mixed. Spread the honey mixture over the plain cookies and top with the nut-coated cookies.

Chapter 4
Sweet Pies & Pastries

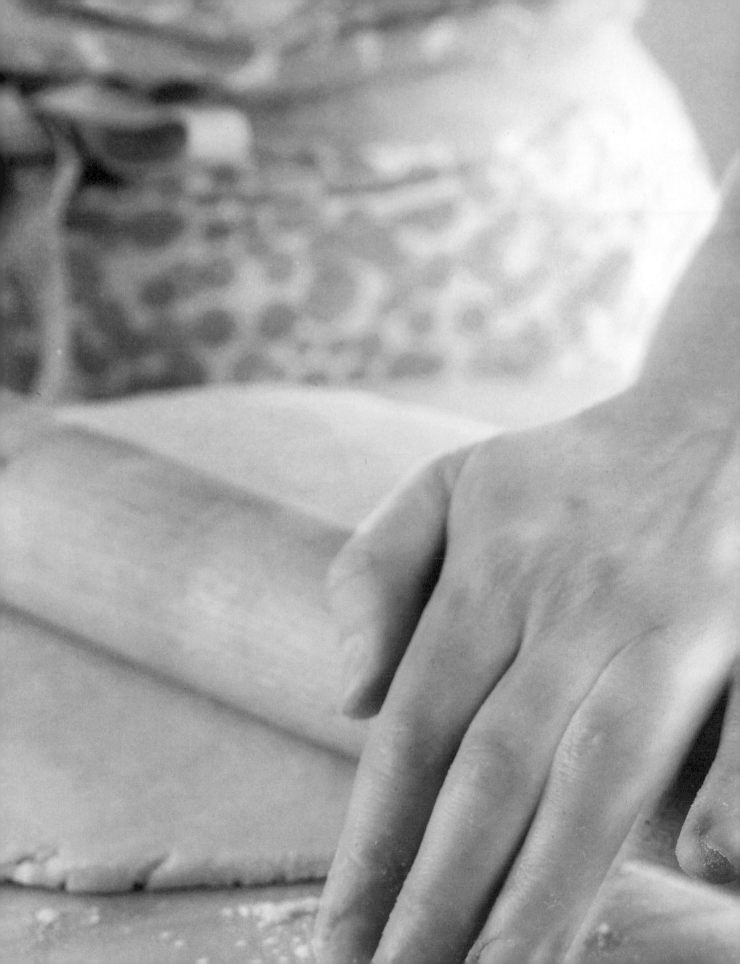

Lemon Meringue Pie

Serves 6

ingredients

pie dough

- scant 1¼ cups all-purpose flour, plus extra for dusting
- 6 tbsp butter, cut into small pieces, plus extra for greasing
- heaping ¼ cup confectioners' sugar, sifted
- finely grated rind of ½ lemon
- ½ egg yolk, beaten
- 1½ tbsp milk

filling

- 3 tbsp cornstarch
- 1¼ cups water
- juice and grated rind of 2 lemons
- heaping ¾ cup superfine sugar
- 2 eggs, separated

1 To make the pie dough, sift the flour into a bowl. Add the butter and cut into the flour, then rub in with your fingertips until the mixture resembles breadcrumbs. Stir in the confectioners' sugar and lemon rind. Stir in the egg yolk and milk and mix to a smooth dough. Shape into a ball, cover, and chill for 30 minutes.

2 Preheat the oven to 350°F/180°C. Grease an 8-inch/20-cm round fluted tart pan with butter. Roll out the pastry on a lightly floured surface to a thickness of ¼ inch/5 mm, then use it to line the bottom and the sides of the pan. Prick all over with a fork, line with parchment paper, and fill with pie weights or dried beans. Bake in the preheated oven for 15 minutes. Remove the pastry shell from the oven and take out the paper and beans. Reduce the oven temperature to 300°F/150°C.

3 For the filling, mix the cornstarch with a little of the water to form a paste. Put the remaining water in a saucepan. Stir in the lemon juice and rind and cornstarch paste. Bring to a boil, stirring. Cook for 2 minutes. Cool a little. Stir in 5 tablespoons of the superfine sugar and the egg yolks, and pour into the pastry shell.

4 Whisk the egg whites in a clean, grease-free bowl until stiff. Gradually whisk in the remaining superfine sugar and spread over the pie. Bake for an additional 40 minutes. Remove from the oven, cool, and serve.

Apple Pie

Serves 6–8

ingredients

pie dough
- 2 cups all-purpose flour
- pinch of salt
- 6 tbsp butter or margarine, cut into small pieces
- 6 tbsp lard or vegetable shortening, cut into small pieces
- about 6 tbsp cold water
- beaten egg or milk, for glazing

filling
- 1 lb 10 oz–2 lb 4 oz/ 750 g–1 kg baking apples, peeled, cored, and sliced
- scant ⅔ cup light brown sugar or superfine sugar, plus extra for sprinkling
- ½–1 tsp ground cinnamon, apple pie spice, or ground ginger
- 1–2 tbsp water (optional)

1 To make the pie dough, sift the flour and salt into a large bowl. Add the butter and lard and rub in using your fingertips until the mixture resembles fine breadcrumbs. Add the water and gather the mixture together into a dough. Wrap the dough and let chill in the refrigerator for 30 minutes.

2 Preheat the oven to 425°F/220°C. Roll out almost two-thirds of the pie dough thinly and use to line a deep 9-inch/23-cm pie plate.

3 For the filling, mix the apples with the sugar and spice and pack into the pastry shell; the filling can come up above the rim. Add the water if needed, particularly if the apples are a dry variety.

4 Roll out the remaining pie dough to form a lid. Dampen the edges of the pie rim with water and position the lid, pressing the edges firmly together. Trim and crimp the edges.

5 Use the trimmings to cut out leaves or other shapes to decorate the top of the pie. Dampen and attach. Glaze the top of the pie with beaten egg or milk, make one or two slits in the top, and place the pie plate on a baking sheet.

6 Bake in the preheated oven for 20 minutes, then reduce the temperature to 350°F/180°C and bake for an additional 30 minutes, or until the pastry is a light golden brown. Serve hot or cold, sprinkled with sugar.

Sweet Pumpkin Pie

Serves 4

ingredients

filling
- 4 lb/1.8 kg pumpkin
- 1¾ cups sweetened condensed milk
- 2 eggs
- 1 tsp salt
- ½ tsp vanilla extract
- 1 tbsp raw sugar

pie dough
- 1 cup all-purpose flour, plus extra for dusting
- ¼ tsp baking powder
- 1½ tsp ground cinnamon
- ¾ tsp ground nutmeg
- ¾ tsp ground cloves
- ¼ cup superfine sugar
- 4 tbsp unsalted butter, chilled and diced, plus extra for greasing
- 1 egg

topping
- 2 tbsp all-purpose flour
- 4 tbsp raw sugar
- 1 tsp ground cinnamon
- 2 tbsp unsalted butter, chilled and diced
- heaping ⅔ cup pecans, chopped
- heaping ⅔ cup walnuts, chopped

1 Preheat the oven to 375°F/190°C. Quarter the pumpkin, remove the seeds, and discard the stem and stringy insides. Place the pumpkin quarters cut-side down in a roasting pan and cover with foil. Bake in the preheated oven for 1½ hours, then remove from the oven and let cool. Scoop out the flesh and puree in a food processor. Drain away any excess liquid and chill until ready to use.

2 To make the pie dough, grease a 9-inch/23-cm pie plate. Sift the flour and baking powder into a bowl. Stir in the spices and the superfine sugar. Rub in the butter until the mixture resembles fine breadcrumbs, then make a well in the center. Beat 1 egg and pour it into the well. Mix together, then use your hands to shape into a ball.

3 Place on a lightly dusted surface and roll out to a circle large enough to line the prepared pie plate. Line the plate and trim the edge. Cover the pie plate with plastic wrap and let chill for 30 minutes.

4 Preheat the oven to 425°F/220°C. To make the filling, place the pumpkin puree in a large bowl, then stir in the condensed milk and the 2 eggs. Add the salt, then stir in the vanilla extract and raw sugar. Pour into the pastry shell and bake in the preheated oven for 15 minutes.

5 Meanwhile, make the topping. Combine the flour, sugar, and cinnamon in a bowl, rub in the butter until crumbly, then stir in the nuts. Remove the pie from the oven and reduce the heat to 350°F/180°C. Sprinkle the topping over the pie, then bake for an additional 35 minutes. Remove from the oven and serve hot or cold.

Mississippi Mud Pie

Serves 12–14

ingredients
crumb crust
- 20 graham crackers (about 5 oz/140 g)
- ¾ cup finely chopped pecans
- 1 tbsp light brown sugar
- ½ tsp ground cinnamon
- 6 tbsp butter, melted

filling
- 1 cup butter or margarine, plus extra for greasing
- 6 oz/175 g bittersweet chocolate
- ½ cup light corn syrup
- 4 extra large eggs, beaten
- ¾ cup finely chopped pecans

1 Preheat the oven to 350°F/180°C. Grease a 9-inch/23-cm springform or loose-bottom round cake pan.

2 To make the crumb crust, put the graham crackers, pecans, sugar, and cinnamon into a food processor and process until fine crumbs form—do not overprocess to a powder. Add the melted butter and process again until moistened.

3 Tip the crumb mixture into the prepared cake pan and press over the bottom and about 1½ inches/4 cm up the sides of the pan. Cover the pan and chill while making the filling.

4 To make the filling, put the butter, chocolate, and corn syrup into a saucepan over low heat and stir until melted and blended. Let cool, then beat in the eggs and pecans.

5 Pour the filling into the chilled crumb crust and smooth the surface. Bake in the preheated oven for 30 minutes, or until just set but still soft in the center. Let cool on a wire rack. Serve at room temperature or chilled.

Latticed Cherry Pie

Serves 8

ingredients

pie dough

- 1 cup all-purpose flour, plus extra for dusting
- ¼ tsp baking powder
- ½ tsp allspice
- ½ tsp salt
- ¼ cup granulated sugar
- 6 tbsp unsalted butter, chilled and diced, plus extra for greasing
- 1 beaten egg, plus extra for glazing

filling

- 2 lb/900 g pitted fresh or canned cherries, drained
- ¾ cup granulated sugar
- ½ tsp almond extract
- 2 tsp cherry brandy
- ¼ tsp allspice
- 2 tbsp cornstarch
- 2 tbsp water

1 To make the pie dough, sift the flour and baking powder into a large bowl. Stir in the allspice, salt, and sugar. Using your fingertips, rub in 4 tablespoons of butter until the mixture resembles fine breadcrumbs, then make a well in the center. Pour the beaten egg into the well. Mix with a wooden spoon, then shape the mixture into a dough. Cut the dough in half and use your hands to roll each half into a ball. Wrap the dough in plastic wrap and let chill for 30 minutes.

2 Preheat the oven to 425°F/220°C. Grease a 9-inch/23-cm pie plate. Roll out the dough into two circles, each 12 inches/30 cm in diameter. Use one to line the prepared pie plate. Trim the edges, leaving an overhang of ½ inch/1 cm.

3 To make the filling, place half the cherries and all the sugar in a large pan. Bring to a simmer over low heat, stirring, for 5 minutes, or until the sugar has melted. Stir in the almond extract, brandy, and allspice. In a separate bowl, mix the cornstarch and water to form a paste. Remove the pan from the heat, stir in the cornstarch, then return to the heat and stir continuously until the mixture boils and thickens. Let cool a little. Stir in the remaining cherries, pour into the pastry shell, then dot with the remaining butter.

4 Cut the remaining dough circle into long strips ½ inch/1 cm wide. Lay five strips evenly across the top of the filling in the same direction, folding back every other strip. Now lay six strips crosswise over the strips, folding back every other strip each time you add another crosswise strip, to form a lattice. Trim off the ends and seal the edges with water. Use your fingers to crimp around the rim, then brush the top with beaten egg.

5 Cover with foil, then bake in the preheated oven for 30 minutes. Remove from the oven, discard the foil, then return the pie to the oven for an additional 15 minutes, or until cooked and golden.

Pecan Pie

Serves 8

ingredients

pie dough
- 1¾ cups all-purpose flour, plus extra for dusting
- ½ cup butter
- 2 tbsp superfine sugar

filling
- 5 tbsp butter
- scant ½ cup light brown sugar
- ⅔ cup light corn syrup
- 2 extra large eggs, beaten
- 1 tsp vanilla extract
- 1 cup pecans

1 For the pie dough, place the flour in a bowl and rub in the butter using your fingertips until it resembles fine breadcrumbs. Stir in the superfine sugar and add enough cold water to mix to a firm dough. Wrap in plastic wrap and chill for 15 minutes, until firm enough to roll out.

2 Preheat the oven to 400°F/200°C. Roll out the dough on a lightly floured surface and use to line a 9-inch/23-cm loose-bottom fluted tart pan. Prick the bottom with a fork. Chill for 15 minutes.

3 Place the tart pan on a cookie sheet and line with a sheet of parchment paper and pie weights or dried beans. Bake in the preheated oven for 10 minutes. Remove the paper and weights and bake for an additional 5 minutes. Reduce the oven temperature to 350°F/180°C.

4 For the filling, place the butter, brown sugar, and corn syrup in a saucepan and heat gently until melted. Remove from the heat and quickly beat in the eggs and vanilla extract.

5 Coarsely chop the pecans and stir into the mixture. Pour into the pie shell and bake in the preheated oven for 35–40 minutes, until the filling is just set. Serve warm or cold.

Cranberry & Almond Tart

Serves 8–10

ingredients

pie dough

- ¼ cup all-purpose flour, plus extra for dusting
- ½ cup superfine sugar
- ½ cup butter, cut into small pieces, plus extra for greasing
- 1 tbsp water

filling

- 1 cup unsalted butter
- 1 cup superfine sugar
- 1 egg
- 2 egg yolks
- 6 tbsp all-purpose flour, sifted
- 1⅔ cups ground almonds
- 4 tbsp heavy cream
- 14½ oz/410 g canned apricot halves, drained
- 1¼ cups fresh cranberries

1 To make the dough, place the flour and sugar in a bowl and rub in the butter with your fingers. Add the water and work the mixture together until a soft pastry has formed. Wrap in plastic wrap and let chill for 30 minutes.

2 On a lightly floured surface, roll out the dough and line a greased 9½-inch/24-cm loose-bottom tart pan. Prick the pastry with a fork and let chill for 30 minutes.

3 Preheat the oven to 375°F/190°C. Line the pastry shell with parchment paper and fill with pie weights or dried beans. Bake in the preheated oven for 15 minutes. Remove the paper and weights and cook for an additional 10 minutes.

4 To make the filling, cream together the butter and sugar until light and fluffy. Beat in the egg and egg yolks, then stir in the flour, almonds, and cream.

5 Place the apricot halves and cranberries on the bottom of the pie shell and spoon the filling over the top.

6 Bake in the preheated oven for about 1 hour, or until the topping is just set. Let cool slightly, then serve warm or cold.

Lemon Tart

Serves 6

ingredients
pie dough
- scant 1⅔ cups all-purpose flour, plus extra for dusting
- 3 tbsp ground almonds
- scant ½ cup butter, diced, plus extra for greasing
- heaping ⅓ cup confectioners' sugar, sifted, plus extra for dusting
- finely grated rind of 1 lemon
- 1 egg yolk, beaten
- 3 tbsp milk
- mascarpone cheese or crème fraîche and fresh raspberries, to serve

filling
- 4 eggs
- 1¼ cups superfine sugar
- juice and finely grated rind of 2 lemons
- ⅔ cup heavy cream

1 To make the pie dough, sift the flour into a bowl. Stir in the ground almonds. Add the butter and cut into the flour, then rub in with your fingertips until the mixture resembles breadcrumbs. Stir in the confectioners' sugar and lemon rind. Stir in the egg yolk and milk and mix to a smooth dough. Shape into a ball, cover, and chill for 30 minutes.

2 Preheat the oven to 350°F/180°C. Grease a 9-inch/23-cm fluted tart pan. Roll out the dough on a lightly floured surface to a thickness of ¼ inch/5 mm and use to line the bottom and sides of the pan. Prick all over with a fork, line with parchment paper and fill halfway with pie weights or dried beans. Bake for 15 minutes in the preheated oven.

3 Remove the pastry shell from the oven and take out the paper and beans. Reduce the oven temperature to 300°F/150°C.

4 To make the filling, crack the eggs into a bowl. Whisk in the sugar, then the lemon juice and rind and cream. Spoon into the pastry shell and bake for 45 minutes. Remove from the oven and let cool. Serve the tart topped with mascarpone or crème fraîche and fresh raspberries and dust with confectioners' sugar.

Ricotta Tart with Chocolate & Walnut

Serves 6

ingredients

pie dough
- heaping ½ cup superfine sugar
- heaping ½ cup unsalted butter, softened
- 2 egg yolks
- finely grated rind of 1 lemon
- 2 cups all-purpose flour

filling
- 4½ oz/125 g semisweet chocolate, broken into pieces
- 1 cup ricotta cheese
- ⅓ cup confectioners' sugar, plus extra for dusting
- 2 tbsp dark rum
- 1 tsp vanilla extract
- ¾ cup finely chopped walnuts

1 Preheat the oven to 350°F/180°C. Place the superfine sugar, butter, egg yolks, and lemon rind in a bowl and beat well to mix evenly.

2 Add the flour and work the mixture with your fingers to make a smooth dough. Wrap the dough in plastic wrap and let rest at room temperature for about 10 minutes.

3 To make the filling, melt the chocolate in a heatproof bowl set over a pan of gently simmering water.

4 Mix together the ricotta, confectioners' sugar, rum, vanilla extract, and walnuts. Stir in the melted chocolate, mixing evenly.

5 Roll out two-thirds of the dough and press into the bottom and sides of a 9-inch/23-cm loose-bottom fluted tart pan. Spoon the ricotta mixture into the pastry shell, smoothing level.

6 Roll out the remaining dough, cut into strips, and arrange over the tart to form a lattice. Place on a baking sheet and bake in the preheated oven for 35–40 minutes, until firm and golden. Serve the tart warm, dusted with confectioners' sugar.

Coconut Tart

Serves 6

ingredients

pie dough
- 9-inch/23-cm precooked tart shell

filling
- 2 eggs
- grated rind and juice of 2 lemons
- 1 cup superfine sugar
- 1¾ cups heavy cream
- 1 cup dry unsweetened coconut

1 Preheat the oven to 350°F/180°C. To make the filling, put the eggs, lemon rind, and sugar in a bowl and beat together for 1 minute.

2 Gently stir in the cream, then the lemon juice and, finally, the coconut.

3 Spread the mixture into the pastry shell, place on a baking sheet, and bake in the preheated oven for 40 minutes, until set and golden. Let cool for about 1 hour to firm up. Serve at room temperature.

Pear Tart with Chocolate Sauce

Serves 8

ingredients

pie dough

- ¾ cup all-purpose flour
- ¼ cup ground almonds
- 5 tbsp margarine, plus extra for greasing
- about 3 tbsp water

filling

- 4 tbsp butter
- 4 tbsp superfine sugar
- 2 eggs, beaten
- 1 cup ground almonds
- 2 tbsp unsweetened cocoa
- a few drops of almond extract
- 14 oz/400 g canned pear halves in natural juice, drained

chocolate sauce

- 4 tbsp superfine sugar
- 3 tbsp light corn syrup
- generous ⅓ cup water
- 6 oz/175 g semisweet chocolate, broken into pieces
- 2 tbsp butter

1 Preheat the oven to 400°F/200°C. Grease an 8-inch/20-cm fluted tart pan.

2 Sift the flour into a mixing bowl and stir in the ground almonds. Rub in the margarine with your fingertips until the mixture resembles breadcrumbs. Add enough of the water to mix to a soft dough. Cover, chill in the freezer for 10 minutes, then roll out and use to line the prepared pan. Prick the bottom with a fork and chill again.

3 To make the filling, beat the butter and sugar until light and fluffy. Beat in the eggs, then fold in the ground almonds, cocoa, and almond extract. Spread the almond mixture in the pastry shell. Thinly slice the pears crosswise, flatten slightly, then arrange the slices on top of the almond mixture, pressing down lightly. Bake in the preheated oven for 30 minutes, or until the filling has risen. Cool slightly and transfer to a serving dish, if you want.

4 To make the chocolate sauce, place the sugar, corn syrup, and water in a saucepan and heat gently, stirring until the sugar dissolves. Boil gently for 1 minute. Remove from the heat, add the chocolate and butter, and stir until melted. Serve with the tart.

Plum Crumble Tart

Serves 8–10

ingredients

pie dough

- 1½ cups all-purpose flour
- 1 tbsp cornstarch
- ½ tsp baking powder
- scant ½ cup butter
- ⅓ cup finely chopped hazelnuts
- scant ¼ cup superfine sugar
- 2–3 tbsp milk

filling

- 14 oz/400 g ripe red plums
- 1 tbsp cornstarch
- 3 tbsp superfine sugar
- finely grated rind of
  1 small orange

1 Preheat the oven to 350°F/180°C and preheat a cookie sheet.

2 Sift the flour, cornstarch, and baking powder into a large bowl and rub in the butter using your fingertips until it resembles fine breadcrumbs. Stir in the hazelnuts and sugar with just enough milk to bind together.

3 Remove about a quarter of the mixture, cover, and place in the refrigerator. Gently knead the remainder together and press into the bottom and sides of an 8-inch/20-cm loose-bottom fluted tart pan.

4 For the filling, halve and pit the plums, cut into quarters, and toss with the cornstarch, sugar, and orange rind. Arrange the plums over the dough.

5 Remove the reserved dough from the refrigerator and, using your fingertips, crumble it over the plums.

6 Place the tart on the cookie sheet and bake in the preheated oven for 40–45 minutes, until lightly browned and bubbling.

Lemon & Passion Fruit Tart

Serves 8

ingredients
pie dough
- scant 1½ cups all-purpose flour, plus extra for dusting
- pinch of salt
- ½ cup unsalted butter, chilled and diced
- ¼ cup confectioners' sugar
- 2 egg yolks blended with 2 tbsp ice-cold water

filling
- 4 passion fruits
- juice and finely grated rind of 1 lemon
- ⅔ cup heavy cream
- 4 tbsp crème fraîche or sour cream
- scant ½ cup superfine sugar
- 2 eggs
- 2 egg yolks

to serve
- confectioners' sugar, to dust
- seeds and pulp from 1 passion fruit

1 For the pie dough, sift the flour and salt into a bowl. Rub in the butter until the mixture resembles fine breadcrumbs. Stir in the confectioners' sugar and blended egg yolk and mix to a dough. Turn onto a floured surface and knead lightly until smooth. Wrap in plastic wrap and chill for 20 minutes.

2 Preheat the oven to 400°F/200°C and preheat a baking sheet. Roll out the pastry on a lightly floured surface and use to line a 9-inch/23-cm loose-bottom fluted tart pan. Chill for 20 minutes.

3 Prick the pastry bottom all over with a fork, line with parchment paper, and fill with pie weights or dried beans. Bake on the preheated baking sheet in the oven for 10 minutes. Remove the paper and weights and return the pastry shell to the oven for another 5 minutes, until light golden. Reduce the oven temperature to 350°F/180°C.

4 For the filling, halve the passion fruits and scoop out the seeds and flesh into a fine-meshed strainer set over a pitcher. Press with the back of a spoon until you have about ¼ cup of juice in the pitcher.

5 In a large bowl, whisk together the passion fruit juice, lemon juice and rind, cream, crème fraîche, superfine sugar, eggs, and egg yolks until smooth. Pour into the pastry shell.

6 Bake in the preheated oven for 30–35 minutes, until the filling has just set. Let cool completely. Serve the tart sliced and dusted with confectioners' sugar, and some passion fruit seeds and pulp.

Pear & Pecan Strudel

Serves 4

ingredients
- 2 ripe pears
- 4 tbsp butter
- 1 cup fresh white breadcrumbs
- heaping ⅓ cup shelled pecans, chopped
- 2 tbsp light brown sugar
- finely grated rind of 1 orange
- 3½ oz/100 g filo dough, thawed if frozen
- 6 tbsp orange blossom honey
- 2 tbsp orange juice
- sifted confectioners' sugar, for dusting

1 Preheat the oven to 400°F/200°C. Peel, core, and chop the pears. Melt 1 tablespoon of the butter in a skillet and gently sauté the breadcrumbs until golden. Transfer the breadcrumbs to a bowl and add the pears, nuts, light brown sugar, and orange rind. Place the remaining butter in a small pan and heat until melted.

2 Set aside one sheet of filo dough, keeping it well wrapped, and brush the remaining filo sheets with a little melted butter. Spoon some of the nut filling onto the first filo sheet, leaving a 1-inch/2.5-cm margin around the edge.

3 Build up the strudel by placing more buttered filo sheets on top of the first, spreading each one with nut filling as you build up the layers. Drizzle the honey and orange juice over the top.

4 Fold the short ends over the filling, then roll up, starting at a long side. Carefully lift onto a baking sheet, with the seam facing up. Brush with any remaining melted butter and crumple the reserved sheet of filo dough around the strudel.

5 Bake in the preheated oven for 25 minutes, or until golden and crisp. Dust with sifted confectioners' sugar and serve warm.

Tart Tatin

Serves 6

ingredients

- 1 cup superfine sugar
- scant ¾ cup unsalted butter
- 1 lb 12 oz/800 g Granny Smith apples
- 12 oz/350 g store-bought puff pastry
- vanilla ice cream, to serve

1 Preheat the oven to 375°F/190°C. Place an 8-inch/20-cm ovenproof skillet over low heat and add the sugar. Melt the sugar until it starts to caramelize, but do not let it burn, then add the butter and stir it in to make a light caramel sauce. Remove from the heat.

2 Peel the apples and cut them into eighths vertically. Core the apples and lay them in the skillet on top of the sauce, cut-side up. They should fill the skillet. If there are any large gaps, add a few more apple pieces. Put the skillet over medium heat and cover. Simmer, without stirring, for about 5–10 minutes, until the apples have soaked up some of the sauce, then remove from the heat.

3 Roll out the pastry so that it will thickly cover the skillet, with extra overhanging the sides. Lay it on top of the apples and tuck the edges down inside between the fruit and the skillet until it is sealed. Don't worry about making it look too neat—it will be turned over before serving.

4 Put the skillet into the preheated oven and bake for 25–35 minutes, checking to make sure the pastry doesn't burn. The pastry should be puffed and golden. Remove from the oven and let rest for 30–60 minutes.

5 To serve, make sure the tart is still a little warm (reheat it on the stove if necessary) and place a plate on top. Carefully turn it over and lift the skillet off. Serve with vanilla ice cream.

Cream Palmiers

Serves 8

ingredients

- ¼ cup granulated sugar
- 8 oz/225 g store-bought puff pastry
- ⅔ cup heavy cream
- 1 tbsp confectioners' sugar, sifted
- few drops vanilla extract
- 2 tbsp strawberry jelly

1 Preheat the oven to 425°F/220°C. Dust a work surface with half of the sugar and roll out the pastry on the sugared surface to a 10 x 12-inch/ 25 x 30-cm rectangle.

2 Sprinkle the rest of the sugar over the pastry and gently roll over it with the rolling pin. Roll the two short sides of the pastry into the center until they meet, moisten the edges that meet with a little water, and press together gently. Cut across the roll into 16 even-size slices.

3 Place the slices, cut-side down, on a dampened baking sheet. Use a rolling pin to flatten each one slightly.

4 Bake in the preheated oven for 15–18 minutes, until crisp and golden brown, turning the palmiers over halfway through cooking so that both sides caramelize. Transfer to a wire rack to cool.

5 Whip the cream, confectioners' sugar, and vanilla extract together until softly peaking. Sandwich the palmiers together with the jelly and whipped cream and serve within 2–3 hours of filling.

Chocolate Parfait
Sandwiches

Serves 4

ingredients

- 3 extra large egg whites
- ⅓ cup superfine sugar
- 5 oz/140 g white chocolate, grated
- 1¾ cups heavy cream, whipped
- 12 oz/350 g store-bought puff pastry
- 2 tbsp melted chocolate, to drizzle

1 To make the parfait, beat the egg whites and the sugar together in a heatproof bowl, then set the bowl over a pan of gently simmering water. Using an electric mixer, beat the whites over the heat until you have a light and fluffy meringue. This will take up to 10 minutes. Remove from the heat, add the chocolate, and keep whisking to cool. Fold in the whipped cream.

2 Spoon the parfait into a shallow, rectangular freezerproof container and freeze for 5–6 hours.

3 Meanwhile, preheat the oven to 350°F/180°C and line a cookie sheet with parchment paper. Roll out the pastry and cut into regular-size rectangles to accommodate a slice of the parfait. Place the pastry rectangles on the sheet and top with another cookie sheet, which will keep the pastry flat but crisp. Bake in the preheated oven for 15 minutes, transfer to a wire rack, and let cool.

4 About 20 minutes before you are ready to serve, remove the parfait from the freezer. When it has softened, cut the parfait into slices and put each slice between two pieces of pastry to make a "sandwich." Drizzle with the melted chocolate.

One Roll Fruit Pie

Serves 8

ingredients

pie dough

- heaping 1 cup all-purpose flour, plus extra for dusting
- scant ½ cup butter, cut into small pieces, plus extra for greasing
- 1 tbsp water
- 1 egg, separated
- crushed sugar cubes, for sprinkling

filling

- 1 lb 5 oz/600 g prepared fruit, such as rhubarb, gooseberries, or plums
- heaping ⅓ cup light brown sugar
- 1 tbsp ground ginger

1 Place the flour in a large bowl, add the butter, and rub it in with your fingertips until the mixture resembles breadcrumbs. Add the water and mix together to form a soft dough. Cover and let chill in the refrigerator for 30 minutes.

2 Preheat the oven to 400°F/200°C. Grease a large cookie sheet. Roll out the dough on a lightly floured surface to a 14-inch/35-cm round. Transfer the round to the prepared cookie sheet and brush with the egg yolk.

3 To make the filling, mix the fruit with the sugar and ground ginger and pile it into the center of the pie dough. Turn in the edges of the dough all the way around. Brush the surface of the dough with the egg white and sprinkle with the crushed sugar cubes.

4 Bake in the preheated oven for 35 minutes, or until golden brown. Transfer to a serving plate and serve warm.

New York Cheesecake

Serves 10

ingredients

- generous ½ cup butter, plus extra for greasing
- 1¼ cups finely crushed graham crackers
- 1 tbsp granulated sugar
- 2 lb/900 g cream cheese
- 1¼ cups superfine sugar
- 2 tbsp all-purpose flour
- 1 tsp vanilla extract
- finely grated zest of 1 orange
- finely grated zest of 1 lemon
- 3 eggs
- 2 egg yolks
- 1¼ cups heavy cream

1 Preheat the oven to 350°F/180°C. Place a small saucepan over low heat, add the butter, and heat until it melts, then remove from the heat, stir in the crushed crackers and granulated sugar, and mix through. Press the cracker mixture tightly into the bottom of a greased 9-inch/23-cm springform cake pan. Bake in the preheated oven for 10 minutes. Remove from the oven and let cool on a wire rack.

2 Increase the oven temperature to 400°F/200°C. With an electric mixer, beat the cream cheese until creamy, then gradually add the superfine sugar and flour and beat until smooth. Increase the speed and beat in the vanilla extract, orange zest, and lemon zest, then beat in the eggs and egg yolks one at a time. Finally, beat in the cream. Scrape any excess from the sides and beaters of the mixer into the mixture. It should be light and fluffy—beat on a faster setting if you need to.

3 Butter the sides of the cake pan and pour in the filling. Smooth the top, transfer to the preheated oven, and bake for 15 minutes, then reduce the temperature to 200°F/100°C and bake for an additional 30 minutes. Turn off the oven and let the cheesecake stand in it for 2 hours to cool and set. Cover and refrigerate overnight.

4 Slide a knife around the edge of the cake then unfasten the pan, cut the cheesecake into slices, and serve.

Chapter 5
Bread & Savory

Crusty White Bread

Makes 1 loaf

ingredients

- 1 egg
- 1 egg yolk
- ¾ –1 cup lukewarm water
- 4½ cups white bread flour, plus extra for dusting
- 1½ tsp salt
- 2 tsp superfine sugar
- 1 tsp active dry yeast
- 2 tbsp butter, diced
- vegetable oil, for brushing

1 Lightly beat together the egg and egg yolk in a measuring cup. Stir in enough lukewarm water to make up to 1¼ cups.

2 Sift the flour and salt together into a bowl and stir in the sugar and yeast. Add the butter and rub it in with your fingertips until the mixture resembles breadcrumbs. Make a well in the center, pour in the egg mixture, and stir well with a wooden spoon until the dough begins to come together, then knead with your hands until it leaves the side of the bowl. Turn out onto a lightly floured surface and knead well for about 10 minutes, until smooth and elastic.

3 Brush a bowl with oil. Shape the dough into a ball, put it into the bowl, and put the bowl into a plastic bag or cover with a damp dish towel. Let rise in a warm place for 1–2 hours, until the dough has doubled in volume.

4 Brush a 7½ x 4½ x 3½-inch/ 19 x 12 x 9-cm loaf pan with oil. Turn out the dough onto a lightly floured surface, punch down with your fist, and knead for 1 minute. With lightly floured hands, shape the dough into a rectangle the same length as the pan and flatten slightly. Fold it lengthwise into three and place in the prepared pan, seam-side down. Put the pan into a plastic bag or cover with a damp dish towel and let rise in a warm place for 30 minutes, until the dough has reached the top of the pan.

5 Preheat the oven to 425°F/220°C. Bake in the preheated oven for 30 minutes, until it has shrunk from the sides of the pan, is golden brown, and sounds hollow when tapped on the bottom with your knuckles. Turn out onto a wire rack to cool.

Whole Wheat
Harvest Bread

Makes 1 small loaf

ingredients

- 2 cups whole wheat bread flour, plus extra for dusting
- 1 tsp salt
- 1 tbsp nonfat dry milk
- 2 tbsp brown sugar
- 1 tsp active dry yeast
- 1½ tbsp vegetable oil, plus extra for brushing
- ¾ cup lukewarm water

1 Sift the flour and salt together into a bowl, tip in the bran from the sifter, and stir in the milk, sugar, and yeast. Make a well in the center and pour in the oil and lukewarm water. Stir well with a wooden spoon until the dough begins to come together, then knead with your hands until it leaves the side of the bowl. Turn out onto a lightly floured surface and knead well for about 10 minutes, until smooth and elastic.

2 Brush a bowl with oil. Shape the dough into a ball, put it into the bowl, and put the bowl into a plastic bag or cover with a damp dish towel. Let rise in a warm place for 1 hour, until the dough has doubled in volume.

3 Brush a 6½ x 4¼ x 3¼-inch/17 x 11 x 8-cm loaf pan with oil. Turn out the dough onto a lightly floured counter, punch down with your fist, and knead for 1 minute. With lightly floured hands, shape the dough into a rectangle the same length as the pan and flatten slightly. Fold it lengthwise into three and place in the prepared pan, seam-side down. Put the pan into a plastic bag or cover with a damp dish towel and let rise in a warm place for 30 minutes, until the dough has reached the top of the pan.

4 Preheat the oven to 425°F/220°C. Bake in the preheated oven for about 30 minutes, until it has shrunk from the sides of the pan, the crust is golden brown, and it sounds hollow when tapped on the bottom with your knuckles. Turn out onto a wire rack to cool.

Chile-Cilantro Naan

Makes 8

ingredients

- 3¼ cups all-purpose flour
- 2 tsp sugar
- 1 tsp salt
- 1 tsp baking powder
- 1 egg
- heaping 1 cup milk
- 2 tbsp sunflower or olive oil, plus extra for brushing
- 2 fresh red chiles, chopped (seeded if you like)
- 1 cup fresh cilantro leaves, chopped
- 2 tbsp butter, melted

1 Sift the flour, sugar, salt, and baking powder together into a large bowl. Whisk the egg and milk together and gradually add to the flour, mixing with a wooden spoon, until a dough is formed.

2 Transfer the dough to a surface, make a depression in the center of the dough, and add the oil. Knead for 3 to 4 minutes, until the oil is absorbed by the flour and you have a smooth and pliable dough. Wrap the dough in plastic wrap and let rest for 1 hour.

3 Divide the dough into 8 equal-size pieces, form each piece into a ball, and flatten into a thick cake. Cover the dough cakes with plastic wrap and let rest for 10–15 minutes.

4 Preheat the broiler on high for 10 minutes, line a broiler pan with a piece of foil, and brush with oil.

5 The traditional shape of naan is teardrop, but you can make them any shape you like. To make the traditional shape, roll each flattened cake into a 5-inch/13-cm diameter round and pull the lower end gently. Carefully roll out again, maintaining the teardrop shape, to about 9 inches/23 cm in diameter. Alternatively, roll the flattened cakes out to 9-inch/23-cm rounds.

6 Mix the chiles and cilantro together, then divide into 8 equal portions and spread each on the surface of a naan. Press gently so that the mixture sticks to the dough. Transfer a naan to the prepared broiler pan and cook 5 inches/13 cm below the heat source for 1 minute, or until slightly puffed and brown patches appear on the surface. Watch carefully, and as soon as brown spots appear on the surface, turn over and cook the other side for 45–50 seconds, until lightly browned. Remove from the broiler and brush with the melted butter. Wrap in a dish towel while you cook the remaining naans.

Tomato & Rosemary
Focaccia

Makes 1 loaf

ingredients
- 4½ cups white bread flour, plus extra for dusting
- 1½ tsp salt
- 1½ tsp active dry yeast
- 2 tbsp chopped fresh rosemary, plus extra sprigs to garnish
- 6 tbsp extra virgin olive oil, plus extra for brushing
- 1½ cups lukewarm water
- 6 sun-dried tomatoes in oil, drained
- 1 tsp coarse sea salt

1 Sift the flour and salt together into a bowl and stir in the yeast and rosemary. Make a well in the center, pour in 4 tablespoons of the oil, and mix quickly with a wooden spoon. Gradually stir in the lukewarm water but do not overmix. Turn out onto a lightly floured surface and knead for 2 minutes. The dough will be quite wet; do not add more flour.

2 Brush a bowl with oil. Shape the dough into a ball, put it into the bowl, and cover with a damp dish towel. Let rise in a warm place for 2 hours, until doubled in volume.

3 Brush a cookie sheet with oil. Turn out the dough onto a lightly floured surface and punch down with your fist, then knead for 1 minute. Put the dough onto the prepared cookie sheet and press out into an even layer. Cover the cookie sheet with a damp dish towel and let rise in a warm place for 1 hour.

4 Preheat the oven to 475°F/240°C. Cut the sun-dried tomatoes into pieces. Whisk the remaining oil with a little water in a bowl. Dip your fingers into the oil mixture and press them into the dough to make indentations all over the loaf. Sprinkle with the sea salt. Press the tomato pieces into some of the indentations, drizzle with the remaining oil mixture, and sprinkle the loaf with the rosemary sprigs.

5 Reduce the oven temperature to 425°F/220°C and bake the focaccia for 20 minutes, until golden brown. Transfer to a wire rack to cool slightly, then serve while still warm.

Herb Focaccia

Makes 1 loaf

ingredients

- 3½ cups white bread flour, plus extra for dusting
- 2¼ tsp active dry yeast
- 1½ tsp salt
- ½ tsp sugar
- 1¼ cups lukewarm water
- 3 tbsp extra virgin olive oil, plus extra for greasing
- ¼ cup finely chopped fresh mixed herbs
- cornmeal, for sprinkling
- sea salt, for sprinkling

1 Combine the flour, yeast, salt, and sugar in a bowl and make a well in the center. Gradually stir in most of the water and 2 tablespoons of the olive oil to make a dough. Gradually add the remaining water, if necessary, drawing in all the flour.

2 Turn out onto a lightly floured surface and knead. Transfer to a bowl and lightly knead in the herbs for 10 minutes, until soft but not sticky. Wash the bowl and lightly coat with olive oil.

3 Shape the dough into a ball, put it in the bowl, and turn the dough over so it is coated. Cover tightly with a dish towel or lightly greased plastic wrap and let rise in a warm place until the dough has doubled in volume. Meanwhile, sprinkle cornmeal over a cookie sheet.

4 Turn the dough out onto a lightly floured surface and knead lightly. Cover with the upturned bowl and let stand for 10 minutes. Meanwhile, preheat the oven to 450°F/230°C.

5 Roll out and pat the dough into a 10-inch/25-cm circle, about ½ inch/ 1 cm thick, and carefully transfer it to the prepared cookie sheet. Cover with a dish towel and let rise again for 15 minutes.

6 Using a lightly oiled finger, poke indentations all over the surface of the loaf. Drizzle over the remaining olive oil and sprinkle lightly with sea salt. Bake in the preheated oven for 15 minutes, or until golden brown and the loaf sounds hollow when tapped on the bottom. Transfer to a wire rack to cool completely.

Flat Bread with Onion & Rosemary

Makes 1 loaf

ingredients

- 4 cups white bread flour, plus extra for dusting
- ½ tsp salt
- 1½ tsp active dry yeast
- 2 tbsp chopped fresh rosemary, plus small sprigs to garnish
- 5 tbsp extra virgin olive oil, plus extra for brushing
- 1¼ cups lukewarm water
- 1 red onion, thinly sliced and pushed out into rings
- 1 tbsp coarse sea salt

1 Sift the flour and salt together into a bowl and stir in the yeast and rosemary. Make a well in the center and pour in 3 tablespoons of the oil and all of the lukewarm water. Stir well with a wooden spoon until the dough begins to come together, then knead with your hands until it leaves the side of the bowl. Turn out onto a lightly floured surface and knead well for about 10 minutes, until smooth and elastic.

2 Brush a bowl with oil. Shape the dough into a ball, put it into the bowl, and put the bowl into a plastic bag or cover with a damp dish towel. Let rise in a warm place for 1 hour, until the dough has doubled in volume.

3 Brush a cookie sheet with oil. Turn out the dough onto a lightly floured surface, punch down with your fist, and knead for 1 minute. Roll out the dough to a round about 12 inches/30 cm in diameter and put it on the prepared cookie sheet. Put the cookie sheet into a plastic bag or cover with a damp dish towel and let rise in a warm place for 20–30 minutes.

4 Preheat the oven to 400°F/200°C. Using the handle of a wooden spoon, make indentations all over the surface of the loaf. Spread the onion rings over the top, drizzle with the remaining oil, and sprinkle with the sea salt. Bake in the preheated oven for 20 minutes. Sprinkle with the rosemary sprigs, return to the oven, and bake for 5 minutes more, until golden brown. Transfer to a wire rack to cool slightly and serve warm.

Irish Soda Bread

Makes 1 loaf

ingredients

- vegetable oil, for brushing
- 4 cups all-purpose flour, plus extra for dusting
- 1 tsp salt
- 1 tsp baking soda
- 1¾ cups buttermilk

1 Preheat the oven to 425°F/220°C. Brush a cookie sheet with oil.

2 Sift the flour, salt, and baking soda together into a bowl. Make a well in the center and pour in most of the buttermilk. Mix well, first with a wooden spoon and then with your hands. The dough should be very soft but not too wet. If necessary, add the remaining buttermilk.

3 Turn out the dough onto a lightly floured surface and knead lightly and briefly. Shape into an 8-inch/20-cm round. Put the loaf onto the prepared cookie sheet and cut a cross in the top with a sharp knife.

4 Bake in the preheated oven for 25–30 minutes, until golden brown and the loaf sounds hollow when tapped on the bottom with your knuckles. Transfer to a wire rack to cool slightly and serve warm.

Bagels

Makes 10

ingredients

- 3 cups white bread flour, plus extra for dusting
- 2 tsp salt
- 2¼ tsp active dry yeast
- 1 tbsp lightly beaten egg
- scant 1 cup lukewarm water
- vegetable oil, for brushing
- 1 egg white
- 2 tbsp water
- 2 tbsp caraway seeds

1 Sift the flour and salt together into a bowl and stir in the yeast. Make a well in the center, pour in the egg and lukewarm water, and mix to a dough. Turn out onto a lightly floured surface and knead well for about 10 minutes, until smooth.

2 Brush a bowl with oil. Shape the dough into a ball, place it in the bowl, and put the bowl into a plastic bag or cover with a damp dish towel. Let rise in a warm place for 1 hour, until the dough has doubled in volume.

3 Brush two cookie sheets with oil and dust a baking sheet with flour. Turn out the dough onto a lightly floured surface and punch down with your fist. Knead for 2 minutes, then divide into 10 pieces. Shape each piece into a ball and let rest for 5 minutes. Gently flatten each ball with a lightly floured hand and make a hole in the center with the handle of a wooden spoon. Put the bagels on the floured sheet, put it into a plastic bag or cover with a damp dish towel, and let rise in a warm place for 20 minutes.

4 Meanwhile, preheat the oven to 425°F/220°C and bring a large pan of water to a boil. Reduce the heat until the water is barely simmering, then add two bagels. Poach for 1 minute, then turn over, and poach for an additional 30 seconds. Remove with a slotted spoon and drain on a dish towel. Poach the remaining bagels in the same way.

5 Transfer the bagels to the oiled cookie sheets. Beat the egg white with the water in a bowl and brush it over the bagels. Sprinkle with the caraway seeds and bake in the preheated oven for 25–30 minutes, until golden brown. Transfer to a wire rack to cool.

English Muffins

Makes 10–12

ingredients

- 4 cups white bread flour, plus extra for dusting
- ½ tsp salt
- 1 tsp superfine sugar
- 1½ tsp active dry yeast
- generous 1 cup lukewarm water
- ½ cup plain yogurt
- vegetable oil, for brushing
- ¼ cup semolina

1 Sift the flour and salt together into a bowl and stir in the sugar and yeast. Make a well in the center and add the lukewarm water and yogurt. Stir with a wooden spoon until the dough begins to come together, then knead with your hands until it comes away from the side of the bowl. Turn out onto a lightly floured surface and knead for 5–10 minutes, until smooth and elastic.

2 Brush a bowl with oil. Shape the dough into a ball, put it into the bowl, and put the bowl into a plastic bag or cover with a damp dish towel. Let rise in a warm place for 30–40 minutes, until the dough has doubled in volume.

3 Dust a cookie sheet with flour. Turn out the dough onto a lightly floured surface and knead lightly. Roll out to a thickness of ¾ inch/2 cm. Stamp out 10–12 rounds with a 3-inch/7.5-cm cookie cutter and sprinkle each round with semolina. Transfer the muffins to the prepared cookie sheet, put it into a plastic bag or cover with a damp dish towel, and let rise in a warm place for 30–40 minutes.

4 Heat a broiler or large skillet over medium–high heat. Add half of the muffins and cook for 7–8 minutes on each side, until golden brown. Cook the remaining muffins in the same way.

5 Let cool and store in an airtight container for up to two days. To serve, split the muffins in half and toast lightly before serving.

Cheese & Chive Bread

Serves 8

ingredients

- heaping 1½ cups self-rising flour
- 1 tsp salt
- 1 tsp dry mustard
- 1 cup grated sharp cheese
- 2 tbsp chopped fresh chives
- 1 egg, lightly beaten
- 2 tbsp butter, melted,
  plus extra for greasing
- ⅔ cup milk

1 Preheat the oven to 375°F/190°C. Grease a 9-inch/23-cm square cake pan and line with parchment paper.

2 Sift the self-rising flour, salt, and dry mustard together into a large mixing bowl.

3 Reserve 3 tablespoons of the grated sharp cheese for sprinkling over the top of the loaf before baking in the oven. Stir the remaining cheese into the bowl along with the chopped fresh chives. Mix well together.

4 Add the beaten egg, melted butter, and milk and stir the mixture thoroughly to combine. Pour the mixture into the prepared pan and spread out evenly with a knife or spatula. Sprinkle over the reserved grated cheese.

5 Bake in the preheated oven for about 30 minutes. Let the bread cool slightly in the pan, then turn out onto a wire rack to cool completely. Cut into triangles to serve.

Olive & Sun-Dried Tomato Bread

Makes 2 loaves

ingredients

- 3½ cups all-purpose flour, plus extra for dusting
- 1 tsp salt
- 2¼ tsp active dry yeast
- 1 tsp brown sugar
- 1 tbsp chopped fresh thyme
- scant 1 cup lukewarm water
- 4 tbsp olive oil, plus extra for brushing
- ½ cup sliced, pitted black olives
- ½ cup sliced, pitted green olives
- 1¾ cups drained sun-dried tomatoes in oil, sliced
- 1 egg yolk, beaten

1 Sift the flour and salt together into a bowl and stir in the yeast, sugar, and thyme. Make a well in the center and pour in the lukewarm water and oil. Stir well with a wooden spoon until the dough begins to come together, then knead with your hands until it leaves the side of the bowl. Turn out onto a lightly floured surface and knead in the olives and sun-dried tomatoes, then knead for an additional 5 minutes, until the dough is smooth and elastic.

2 Brush a bowl with oil. Shape the dough into a ball, put it into the bowl, and put the bowl into a plastic bag or cover with a damp dish towel. Let rise in a warm place for 1–1½ hours, until the dough has doubled in volume.

3 Dust a cookie sheet with flour. Turn out the dough onto a lightly floured surface and punch down with your fist. Cut it in half and with lightly floured hands, shape each half into a round or oval. Put them on the prepared cookie sheet and put the cookie sheet into a plastic bag or cover with a damp dish towel. Let rise in a warm place for 45 minutes.

4 Preheat the oven to 400°F/200°C. Make three shallow diagonal slashes on the top of each loaf and brush with the beaten egg yolk. Bake in the preheated oven for 40 minutes, until golden brown and the loaves sound hollow when tapped on the bottom with your knuckles. Transfer to a wire rack to cool.

Brioche Braid

Makes 1 loaf

ingredients

- 2½ cups white bread flour, plus extra for dusting
- ½ tsp salt
- ½ cup unsalted butter, chilled and diced, plus extra for greasing
- 2 tbsp superfine sugar
- 2¼ tsp active dry yeast
- 2 eggs, beaten
- generous ¼ cup warm milk
- olive oil, for greasing
- beaten egg, to glaze

1 Sift the flour and salt into a large mixing bowl. Add the butter and rub into the flour with your fingertips. Stir in the sugar and yeast. Make a well in the center.

2 Pour the eggs and milk into the bowl. Stir well to make a soft dough. Turn the dough onto a lightly floured surface and knead for 5–10 minutes, until the dough is smooth and elastic, sprinkling with a little more flour if the dough becomes sticky.

3 Grease a large baking sheet. Divide the dough into 3 equal pieces and shape each into a rope about 14 inches/35 cm long. Place the ropes side by side and press them together at one end. Braid the ropes, then pinch the ends together.

4 Transfer the braid to the prepared baking sheet, cover loosely with oiled plastic wrap, and let stand in a warm place for about 1 hour, until almost doubled in size.

5 Preheat the oven to 375°F/190°C. Brush the braid with the beaten egg. Bake in the preheated oven for 30–35 minutes, until risen and golden brown, covering loosely with foil after 25 minutes to prevent it from becoming too brown. Serve warm.

Tomato & Basil Muffins

Makes 12

ingredients

- sunflower oil, for greasing
- 2 cups all-purpose flour
- 1 tbsp baking powder
- pinch of salt
- ⅔ cup finely chopped, drained sun-dried tomatoes in oil (oil reserved)
- 2 eggs
- generous 1 cup buttermilk
- ¼ cup chopped fresh basil leaves
- 1 garlic clove, crushed
- 2 tbsp freshly grated Parmesan cheese
- freshly ground black pepper

1 Preheat the oven to 400°F/200°C. Grease a 12-hole muffin pan. Sift together the flour, baking powder, salt, and pepper to taste into a large bowl. Stir in the sun-dried tomatoes.

2 Place the eggs in a large pitcher or bowl and beat lightly, then beat in the buttermilk, 6 tablespoons of the reserved oil from the tomatoes, the basil, and garlic. Make a well in the center of the dry ingredients and pour in the beaten liquid ingredients. Stir gently until just combined; do not overmix. Spoon the batter into the prepared muffin pan. Scatter the Parmesan cheese over the tops of the muffins.

3 Bake in the preheated oven for 20 minutes, or until well risen, golden brown, and firm to the touch. Let cool in the pan for 5 minutes, then serve warm.

Chile Cornbread Muffins

Makes 12

ingredients

- 1¼ cups all-purpose flour
- 4 tsp baking powder
- 1¼ cups cornmeal
- 2 tbsp superfine sugar
- 1 tsp salt
- 4 scallions, trimmed and finely chopped
- 1 red chile pepper, seeded and finely chopped
- 3 eggs, beaten
- ⅔ cup plain yogurt
- ⅔ cup milk

1 Preheat the oven to 400°F/200°C. Put 12 baking cups in a muffin pan.

2 Sift the flour and baking powder into a large bowl. Stir in the cornmeal, sugar, salt, scallions, and chile pepper. Beat together the eggs, yogurt, and milk, then pour into the flour mixture and beat until just combined. Spoon the mixture into the baking cups.

3 Bake the muffins in the preheated oven for 15–20 minutes, until risen, golden, and just firm to the touch. Serve warm.

Walnut & Romano Biscuits

Makes about 16

ingredients
- 3¼ cups self-rising flour, plus extra for dusting
- pinch of salt
- 6 tbsp butter, diced, plus extra for greasing
- ¼ cup superfine sugar
- ½ cup grated Romano cheese
- 1 cup walnut pieces
- about 1¼ cups milk
- butter, to serve

1 Preheat the oven to 400°F/200°C. Grease a baking sheet. Sift the flour and salt into a large bowl. Add the butter and rub it in with your fingertips until the mixture resembles fine breadcrumbs. Stir in the sugar, cheese, and walnuts. Stir in enough of the milk to bring the mixture together into a soft dough.

2 Gently roll the dough out on a lightly floured work surface until it is about 1–1¼ inches/2.5–3 cm thick. Cut out rounds with a 2½-inch/6-cm round cookie cutter (make the biscuits smaller or larger if you prefer). Place the rounds on the prepared baking sheet.

3 Bake in the preheated oven for 15 minutes, or until golden brown and firm to the touch. Transfer to a wire rack to cool. Serve with butter.

Cheese & Mustard Biscuits

Makes 8

ingredients

- 1⅔ cups self-rising flour, plus extra for dusting
- 1 tsp baking powder
- pinch of salt
- 3½ tbsp butter, cut into pieces, plus extra for greasing
- heaping 1 cup grated sharp cheddar cheese
- 1 tsp dry mustard
- ⅔ cup milk, plus extra for brushing
- pepper
- cheese and butter, to serve

1 Preheat the oven to 425°F/220°C. Lightly grease a baking sheet. Sift the flour, baking powder, and salt into a large bowl. Add the butter and rub it in with your fingertips until the mixture resembles breadcrumbs. Stir in the cheese, mustard, and enough milk to form a soft dough.

2 Knead the dough very lightly on a floured work surface, then flatten it out into a round with the palm of your hand to a thickness of about 1 inch/2.5 cm.

3 Cut the dough into eight wedges with a knife. Brush each one with a little milk and sprinkle with pepper to taste. Place the wedges on the prepared baking sheet.

4 Bake in the preheated oven for 10–15 minutes, or until golden brown. Transfer to a wire rack to cool slightly before serving spread with butter and filled with cheese.

Asparagus & Cheese Tart

Serves 6

ingredients
- flour, for dusting
- butter, for greasing
- 9 oz/250 g store-bought flaky pie dough, thawed if frozen
- 9 oz/250 g asparagus
- 1 tbsp vegetable oil
- 1 red onion, finely chopped
- 2 tbsp chopped hazelnuts
- 1 cup goat cheese
- 2 eggs, beaten
- 4 tbsp light cream
- salt and pepper

1 On a lightly floured surface, roll out the pie dough and line a greased, 9½-inch/24-cm loose-bottom fluted tart pan. Prick the bottom of the tart shell with a fork and chill in the refrigerator for 30 minutes. Meanwhile, preheat the oven to 375°F/190°C.

2 Line the tart shell with parchment paper and pie weights or dried beans and bake in the preheated oven for about 15 minutes. Remove the paper and weights and bake for another 15 minutes. Do not turn the oven off.

3 Meanwhile, cook the asparagus in boiling water for 2–3 minutes, drain, and cut into bite-size pieces.

4 Heat the oil in a small skillet. Add the onion and cook over low heat, stirring occasionally, for about 5 minutes, until soft and lightly golden. Spoon the asparagus, onion, and hazelnuts into the prepared tart shell, spreading them out evenly.

5 Beat together the cheese, eggs, and cream until smooth, or process in a blender until smooth. Season well with salt and pepper, then pour the mixture over the asparagus, onion, and hazelnuts.

6 Bake the tart for an additional 15–20 minutes, or until the cheese filling is just set. Serve warm or cold.

Bacon, Onion & Parmesan Tart

Serves 6

ingredients

- 9 oz/250 g store-bought flaky pie dough
- flour, for dusting
- 2½ tbsp butter
- 2¾ oz/75 g bacon, chopped
- 3 large onions, peeled and thinly sliced
- 2 eggs, beaten
- scant ⅛ cup grated Parmesan cheese
- 1 tsp dried sage
- salt and pepper

1 Roll out the pie dough on a lightly floured surface and line a 9½-inch/24-cm loose-bottom fluted tart pan.

2 Prick the bottom of the pie dough with a fork and let chill for 30 minutes.

3 Heat the butter in a pan, add the chopped bacon and sliced onions, and sweat them over low heat for about 25 minutes, or until tender. If the onion slices start to brown, add 1 tablespoon of water to the pan. Meanwhile, preheat the oven to 350°F/180°C.

4 Add the beaten eggs to the onion mixture and stir in the cheese, sage, and salt and pepper to taste.

5 Spoon the filling into the prepared tart shell.

6 Bake in the preheated oven for 20–30 minutes, or until the tart has just set. Let cool slightly in the pan, then serve warm or cold.

Potato & Red Onion Pie

Serves 6

ingredients
- butter, for greasing
- 3 large potatoes, thinly sliced
- 2 scallions, finely chopped
- 1 red onion, finely chopped
- ⅔ cup heavy cream
- 1 lb/450 g store-bought puff pastry
- 2 eggs, beaten
- salt and pepper

1 Preheat the oven to 400°F/200°C. Lightly grease a cookie sheet. Bring a pan of water to a boil, then add the sliced potatoes. Bring back to a boil and simmer for 2–4 minutes. Drain the potato slices and let cool. Dry off any excess moisture with paper towels.

2 In a bowl, mix together the scallions, red onion, and the cooled potato slices. Stir in 2 tablespoons of the cream and plenty of salt and pepper.

3 Divide the pastry in half and roll out one piece to a 9-inch/23-cm circle. Roll the remaining pastry to a 10-inch/25-cm circle.

4 Place the smaller circle onto the prepared cookie sheet and top with the potato mixture, leaving a 1-inch/2.5-cm border. Brush this border with a little of the beaten egg.

5 Top with the larger circle of pastry, seal well, and crimp the edges of the pastry. Cut a steam vent in the middle of the pastry and mark with a pattern. Brush with some of the beaten egg and bake in the preheated oven for 30 minutes.

6 Mix the remaining beaten egg with the remaining cream and pour into the pie through the steam vent. Return to the oven for 15 minutes, then let cool for 30 minutes. Serve warm or cold.